I AM
in-di-vid-u-al
One person, task, or action
Acting alone for the benefit of "I" and/or "We"

WE ARE
In-di-vid-u-al
Many individuals, tasks, or actions
Acting together as ONE for the benefit of "We" and/or "I"

I HAVE
in-flu-ence
My greatest responsibility is
how I affect others with all I do or say.

Individual Influence

Find the "I" in Team

Brian Smith PhD and Mary Griffin

MADE FOR
SUCCESS

Made for Success Publishing
P.O. Box 1775 Issaquah, WA 98027
www.MadeForSuccessPublishing.com

Distributed by Made for Success Publishing

First Printing

Library of Congress Cataloging-in-Publication data
Smith, Brian and Griffin, Mary
    INDIVIDUAL INFLUENCE: Find the "I" in Team
    Book 1 in *The "I" in Team* Series

       p. cm.

LCCN: 2021942682
ISBN: 978-1-64146-720-9 (*Hardback)*
ISBN: 978-1-64146-721-6 (*eBook)*
ISBN: 978-1-64146-722-3 (*Audiobook)*

Printed in the United States of America

For further information contact Made for Success Publishing
+14255266480 or email service@madeforsuccess.net

TABLE OF CONTENTS

Mary's Preface

I can honestly say that beginning to write this series came at the perfect time in my life. This book has helped me on my journey to live more intentionally, be present in the moment, and appreciate the good and the bad. Each of us is experiencing life in a vastly different way from the person next to us; we have different experiences, personalities, habits, morals, and beliefs—there are more things than can be named that make us all individual. To me, this is one of the most beautiful parts of humanity, our diversity. However, every person in this world has one thing in common: We are all human.

To be human is to be given the opportunity to positively influence our world. Much of the positive influence we have is passive, like a smile or positive acknowledgment to a stranger. To share our positive influence through writing is an even greater gift. Telling stories to teach or provoke laughter, sadness, anger, and even frighten, is a tradition older than recorded history. We communicate through stories that tap into these emotions, and our influence comes from the effect we have on others. We can communicate through emotion regardless of the boundaries of language. While this book communicates through pragmatism, it is embedded with stories saturated with the emotions we all feel throughout life. This book capitalizes on the tradition of storytelling to teach, guide, develop, challenge, and influence.

Individual Influence: Find the "I" in Team influences through lessons and philosophies tethered to stories full of raw emotion. Brian and I have created a book in which you can see parts of the real human experience and what we have learned from the battles we all face. We dive into some of life's most challenging questions: "Who am I?" and "What is my purpose here?" We will guide you and support you as you ponder and perhaps even answer these questions for yourself.

Having the ability to learn from others' challenges, failures, and successes is a privilege most of us take for granted. There have been many instances when I have learned from the experiences of others, and I am certain that others have learned from mine as well. While you may have picked up this book thinking it would be a conventional self-help book or business guide, you will be surprised to find that it is so much more.

I have found that too often in self-help books, I am instructed on what I need to do in order to get to a generally outlined destination, and I am told what I am doing wrong with my life. In my experience, self-help books only provide an answer to questions or a solution to problems that we may face; they do not always show us the means by which they came to these conclusions or help us think about how to apply them to our unique situation. This way of teaching is superb in some areas of learning, but for the complexities of human experience, it does not measure up. Context matters.

Our lives are far too dynamic individually, let alone when you consider the billions of other experiences that humankind has every day. We have been learning from one another for many millennia through stories, but only if we choose to listen and apply ourselves. This book brings us back to that type of learning: the learning needed to understand and comprehend some of life's greatest questions.

As the daughter of someone who not only lives by these philosophies but also teaches them, I have a great advantage. Some of Brian's colleagues have described me as a "case study" for this book.

What I have learned from my dad and his teachings goes far beyond anything I could put into words. He has taught me how to love, forgive, move on, have grace, be fierce, stand up for what I believe in, be a great team member, and hold myself accountable. Above all else—and what I truly cherish most—he has taught me how to empathize.

I was lost for so long before we started writing this series. The kind of lost where you honestly believe you may never find yourself again. The kind of lost that makes you question who you are and what you're really doing here. Being a part of the writing of this book and series has helped me find myself again. It allowed me to rediscover my foundation, the foundation my parents spent so long and worked so hard to build for me as a child. It allowed me to focus on my life's mission: to make this world a better place for all living beings.

The benefits you will get from this book go beyond the excitement of reading stories that provoke various emotions; you will have the opportunity to learn and better yourself. You will be able to analyze yourself more clearly and with less bias. This book will prepare you to be your best self with each team you influence: family, friends, coworkers, and strangers. Only you have the power to decide to change your mind and grow into the person you want to be. You can do anything and be anyone. We only ask that whoever you choose to be, you choose to be a positive influence in this world. For you and those you influence, I wish a prosperous life.

ACKNOWLEDGEMENTS

I was unsure where this book project would take me. The title changed a few times as we got deeper into the concept. As the first book of many, this is a testament to our philosophy: all individuals matter. I chose the title *Individual Influence* based on the premise that all individuals matter and that we each have influence; our influence is our single greatest responsibility. I wouldn't have been able to start or finish this project without the influence of our amazing team; their support inspired me, propelled me, and influenced me in too many ways to write. Our company, IA Business Advisors (IA = Individual Advantages), is so named because each individual's influence is the result of their advantages. Our company continues to be positively influenced by those who exude our core philosophies, which we intend to pass on to you in this book. Our core purpose is to find what makes each individual unique and encourage them to use their influence to their advantage.

I owe thanks to my family for everything in my business life. My wife, René—my rock since the day we met—influences me to be honest and work hard, and the pride this instills in me gets me through each day. Our success as businesspeople, parents, and friends is grounded in our partnership, marriage, and friendship.

Our three children grew to be a part of that rock, too. Kristin, my eldest, is one of my inspirations; she repeated many of the lessons I learned throughout life and managed to create an amazing life for her family, as I did for mine. My granddaughter, Kenzi, is a tremendous source of pride for me, and Kristin's husband, Isaiah, is someone I am proud to call family.

Henry, my youngest, is incredibly stubborn. Through it all, he has remained true to his personal beliefs. Henry is as individual as they come yet still manages to be there for anyone lucky enough to be part of his life. Then there is Mary, my middle child. We wrote this book together. Yes, the majority of the thoughts and stories are personal to my history and experience, but without Mary, this book would not exist. It has been a pure joy to work with her, and I look forward to whatever the future holds as we continue to develop the lessons in these pages through *The "I" in Team* series.

Recognizing those who have helped me get here doesn't repay all that I owe them. Their efforts are unparalleled. While attending law school and working a full-time job, Spencer read and reread this book to ensure its lessons were cohesive and clear. Braden provided amazing insight and challenged me to dig deeper into my thoughts and memories to ensure that the lessons resonated with my intention in order to leave a positive influence on each reader. Sarah and Jerrod read and reviewed chapters and provided context and imagery that will bring a little visual connection with the words.

I also recognize my parents and siblings. First, my mother has been a positive influence on my life since high school. Prior to high school, I think our lives were just organized chaos created by young parents struggling to raise young children. Today, my mother is one of my best friends, and her husband, Jeff, is the father to me that every person deserves. My biological father and stepmother certainly influenced who I am, but we have not had anything close to a parent-child relationship since the late '80s. I am happy that their marriage has lasted to this day, and they successfully raised a new family of their own.

My siblings, Becky, Justin, Brandt, and Alexandra, have all influenced the world in their own ways. Becky, with whom I share both parents, is a good friend, and she and Chris (my brother-in-law) are truly amazing people. I don't really know my other siblings well, as they are my stepmother and father's children, but I am delighted to know that they are all successful and happy in their own ways.

To name the remaining individuals who have influenced me on the journey to writing this book would take a book of its own. In fact, several people in my stories in this book have influenced me in my lifetime and contributed to the lessons that have made me a better individual. I am eternally grateful for the good and bad that has happened. They have provided me with the opportunity to create a book of lessons taught through stories that may become part of your own individual influence. I hope they will help you find the "I" in your team.

INTRODUCTION

"The most difficult thing is the decision to act, the rest is merely tenacity. The fears are paper tigers. You can do anything you decide to do. You can act to change and control your life; and the procedure, the process, is its own reward."
—Amelia Earhart

This book will be a journey focused solely on finding yourself. As you will see, each of us is (or should be) the most important person to ourselves; we cannot be the best for others without first being our best self.

We will map this journey and explore the advantages of the individual. Our philosophy is that the word *individual* has dual meanings: one person/many persons, one action/many actions, one word/many words. One is an individual; collectively, they are Individual. Throughout this book, you will notice the use of this term, the subtle differences in its usage, and the way we write the word *(I)individual*. When referring to a single person, task, or action, the word *individual*—with a lowercase *i*—will be used. When referring to an entity made of multiple individuals, the word *Individual*—with a capital *I*—will be used. Finally, if there is a commingling of singular individuals with multiple Individuals or an entity, you will see the spelling *(I)individual.*

There is another word that I am notorious for using, even when it seems I am clearly speaking about myself alone: we. I have been known for using the word *we* to speak about my own accomplishments. This is because there hasn't been anything in my professional career that I have done on my own; I've always had a team supporting me. From my education (both formal and through experience), to the support I get in the office, from partners and vendors, or from my family, there is always a *we* for me. The habit of recognizing my teams ((I)individuals) has provided a positive and successful working relationship with people around the world for over 30 years. To this day, I still correspond and work with people who were peers, partners, vendors, employees, and customers back when I began my career journey. I am *we*, and all that I have become is due to the *we* in my life. What about your life: Who is *your* we?

This is not another self-help book that leaves you wondering, *Can I really do this?* There are no disclaimers such as "results are atypical." Instead, this book is about self-realization (individual realization). It can only fail you if you fail to be honest with yourself. Other books require you to measure up to others: make more money, be more successful, lose more weight, or be a better spouse or person. *Individual Influence* is about how you influence others and how others influence you; those results are subjective. It's about understanding yourself and your (I)individual influences, not about measuring yourself against others or some generally accepted attribute. If you apply the concepts in this book, you will gain new insight into how your personal advantages and strengths influence other individuals and how they influence you; you will have the ability to influence and manage change with any (I)individual in your life.

We will also challenge your personal definition of prosperity. Prosperity, as defined generally today, refers to certain forms of wealth: financial, emotional, romantic, platonic, professional, or educational. For me, prosperity is none of these things. In fact, I have met people who don't have any of the aforementioned wealth who feel prosperous, and I have met people with all of them who are still not satisfied with their place in life (they do not feel prosperous, yet they are surrounded by what others perceive as wealth). Prosperity is personal and is part of the *Individual Influence* approach that you will come to understand by the end of this book.

We intend to give you the tools necessary to learn and apply the philosophies taught here as well as how to apply the philosophies you have learned in the past. How many books/seminars/videos/podcasts have you read/been to/watched/listened to? How many years have you been trying to better yourself or your company through these media and seen little to no improvement? I don't say this to disparage the great work done by people who have developed or identified ways by which others can make themselves better. However, many of the programs, practices, or philosophies being taught don't resonate beyond the initial excitement of hearing or reading about the success of others.

It is also important to know that we will be asking you to look at yourself without rose-colored glasses—meaning using a more objective thought process. You cannot be your best for others if you are not first best for yourself, which means being honest with yourself. Too often, we make excuses that we think are only detrimental to ourselves; but every time we lie or consciously allow ourselves to fall short of personal goals, we chip away at the person who is an advantage to everyone we individually influence. Self-realization, which we will guide you toward, may be difficult. You will see how, for me, it opened memories I had long suppressed. If those memories cause you anxiety or other negative feelings, seriously think about sharing them with someone you trust, or maybe a psychologist; to realize your full individual influence, you will have to understand the foundation of who you are.

This act of self-reflection will demand a thoughtful approach, as it requires you to be truthful to yourself. For new things that require more than intuitive knowledge, the only way to gain complete understanding is to slow down. During these times of self-reflection, we may experience fear of learning. We are humbled by what we uncover about ourselves; to know our truth is to remove those rose-colored glasses and identify those barriers that have been getting in our way.

Chapter 1

Meet Individual Advantages

Let me begin by sharing the story of how Individual Advantages (IA) became what it is today. Individual Advantages has been the name of our company since 1996. The inspiration for the name has escaped many people through the years, including my wife René. In fact, she recently told me that she misunderstood the name for the first 21 years of our company's existence. This revelation came during one of our morning coffee conversations while we were discussing this very book.

While I have always passionately understood the meaning behind our company name, we have often struggled to have a clear public identity because of it. Countless people have said to me, "Why don't you come up with a better company name than 'Individual Advantages'?" Even more frustrating was the confusion when I explained what Individual Advantages was: *A company that helps other companies understand the correlation between people, process, and technology, and the advantages each of these (I)individually has within the workplace.* Looking back on this explanation, it still makes sense to me, though now I understand why people would look at me with confusion in their eyes for so many years.

In those early years, I found it difficult to create our best public image while still keeping the true meaning of IA. For me, Individual Advantages was never about a name but about my belief in what actually makes companies viable: the (I)individual and the influence each has. Through the years, I played around with names and logos that I hoped would help our clients and potential clients realize who we are and what we do. In doing so, we continued to apply our tried-and-true approach to solving the (I)individual business problems posed to us by clients and influencing them in a positive way to the end result.

The other names we tried never captured the true message of IA; in fact, I felt those names lost a certain amount of who we were as an organization. In the mid-2000s, we tried Business Efficiency Group. That name said who we are and that we help businesses but it did not express our beliefs about (I)individuals or the influence they have. In 2009, we again tried a new brand: YourBizDr.Com. The success of this brand was amazing and paved the way for me to share the true value of who we have always attempted to be: a positive influence to the many (I)individuals we have been blessed to work with.

The name YourBizDr.Com came from my close friend Kevin, who called me the "Biz Doctor" and suggested that we apply our practices via virtual services to more people. So, we did. From 2009 to 2014, we helped over 18,000 business owners, managers, and employees realize their (I)individual influence through our virtual services. However, each time I found our company coming back to our foundation of work: helping (I)individuals realize their influence. Working with people to better understand themselves, their organization, and their teams often necessitates deep human interaction. To understand and advise on the complexities of people and organizations requires more than simply answering questions through a chat box or email. So, I reverted my individual work to face-to-face and conventional brick-and-mortar consulting services.

In 2014, when we had the opportunity to sell our virtual consultancy, I was relieved. It's hard to consult with such a large group of clients and influence viable change over the internet through hundreds of disconnected (I)individuals. As an advisory firm, I prefer IA to work shoulder to shoulder helping our clients understand their (I)individual influence and that of their individuals, departments, divisions, or company. That sale has positively influenced our ability to bring *The "I" in Team* series to the world.

In 2017, I finally listened to my team and we changed the name of our consulting operations group from Individual Advantages to IA Business Advisors. For years, our clients referred to us as IA, and I appreciate the simplicity it offers our team and our clients. Today, IA is an organization that influences thousands of (I)individuals around the world while being comprised of hundreds of (I)individuals whose primary goal is to positively influence our clients.

Professional (I)individual influence, as you can see, has been a journey for me, my family, and the (I)individuals who have worked with me these past 30 years. Defining your individual influence will be a journey for you, too. Our goal is that you will take away from this book a plethora of individual advantages, the most significant being that *you* are the single most important individual in this world; your influence matters. It is through you that other individual influences are created.

What are (I)individual Advantages?

So, what exactly are individual advantages and how do they create influence? Well, each of us is individually part of something that is also Individual. (Remember earlier when I discussed the use of lowercase *i* and capital *I* "individual?") For example, a group of individuals creates one Individual family, a group of individuals creates one Individual country, and a group of individuals creates one Individual world. One individual is part of multiple Individuals; a child is part of one Individual family, but that child is also part of one Individual class at school.

As individuals, we each have our own advantages, and through the influences in our life, we can create advantages for other (I)individuals. Our influence creates advantages for everyone we interact with. For example, I am particularly good at mediating complex disagreements, which is an individual advantage to me and to anyone who asks for help resolving complex interpersonal issues. This individual advantage is a result of the influences of my past and the people who contributed to that influence. Other advantages can be your ability to learn, communicate, or perform physical tasks. Individual advantages are our strengths, awareness, areas for growth, and more. Advantages are what we know to be true about ourselves, but we may not realize all our advantages; they are the things we inherently own and can work to improve in order to give our best selves to our work. An example of not realizing our advantages is when we influence others or a situation without actively trying to; often times, we don't know what influence we have or if it's advantageous to others. When we work with others, we become an Individual working toward achieving a singular goal. Each day is made up of interactions between and among many (I)individuals, and it is this choreographed task of communications, decisions, and actions that creates the individual advantages that propel us in life.

In this book, we will help you to identify your internal advantages and how they produce opportunities to influence and create external advantages for other (I)individuals. Advantages and the influence they have are the culmination and result of who we are in any given moment. So, if advantages are innate or created by us, either individually or collectively as an Individual, what are they?

Are advantages something we can use physically? Yes. Like being tall or strong.

Are advantages something we can trade? Yes. In part, that is what all work is; we are all trading our skills—our advantages—to complete goals, tasks, or other various jobs for team members or clients. In a way, you barter your advantages.

To simplify: If you are empathetic and someone needs help navigating a tough emotional situation, you can coach them to be positive using your skill of empathy while also helping them learn. Your act of kindness may influence that individual to share their strengths with you or others when the time comes. However, should we fail to find those who have the advantages to supplement our areas of weakness or learn in a timely manner what we need to succeed, we may find that we fail ourselves.

Failure can also be an advantage. Failure is something we learn from, and it teaches us lessons about whatever caused the failure and what comes next. Failure creates opportunities, which can become our advantage. Failure is a way to learn, grow, and not repeat the past. Learning is an external advantage that we must look out for in order to continue growing our strengths and understanding our room for improvement. In this way, failure is an advantage because it demonstrates our ability to try, grow, and try again. Advantages can propel us forward in life, but they can also hold us back when we do not choose to learn from them as opportunities.

Think of advantages as capital to be used with other (I)individuals. Some people are born into money; one of their advantages is that they do not worry about how to pay for things like education or material items. These individuals may appear to have more advantages than a child who is born into a family who is experiencing financial struggles. However, the lives of these *perceptively* advantaged and disadvantaged people are not necessarily defined by money. Money can be a benefit, just as lack of money can be. It all depends on how the individual chooses to use their influence to grow and be who they want to be. Additionally, not all advantages are identified by generally perceived value.

Affluent children may face challenges such as drugs or envy. They may grow up to be pretentious or sheltered from certain things that could provide them with the necessary tools to learn. They may feel the need to keep their affluence and make decisions that will destroy them emotionally or, at some point, physically. Poor children, while lacking money, may have the benefit of a family or community that teaches them the values that brought them into this world. They may learn how to be more resourceful because of this lack of money. They may also learn about need through hunger or other physical challenges. Going through these challenges can create advantages for them, such as the inspiration and drive to become something more, should they choose to recognize those opportunities. They may yearn for an education instead of taking it for granted. That yearning is an advantage that propels them to grow. Most advantages—empathy, patience, friendship, and maturity, to name a few—come from within and are far more valuable than money.

We are going to explore your individual advantages and how you can use them in the most positive way possible to influence your own life and the lives of others. Quite literally, everything we say, do, create, think, feel, and pass on to others can become an advantage for us and those we influence. This is because every action or lack of action is influential. Everything you put out into the world provides the opportunity for learning and growth.

To help you identify your advantages and how they influence others, we will start with the process of self-reflection—being honest with ourselves. Identification of the individual we have total control over (ourselves) will lead us to understand our ability to influence the (I)individuals we interact with daily. Our influence determines our ability to be successful within the areas where we choose to be active. We hope to help you define your individual advantages, the influence you have over (I)individuals, and the individual advantages you bring to them.

Key Takeaways: What are (I)individual Advantages?

- Lowercase i "individual" = singular (you). We are all individual, we are all an advantage, and we can create advantages.

- Capital I "Individual" = plural (team, group, company, family, community, etc.). When individuals come together with one-to-many other individuals, we form a larger Individual. As an Individual, we create opportunities for more advantages together. Nobody can say who they are without the influence of other individuals.

- Advantages are inherent in who we are as individuals and what we create when we come together as an Individual. Advantages are our skills and attributes—a result of who we are (I)individually.

Opportunities vs. Advantages

How many times have you looked back at your life, an hour, week, month, or even years later, and said to yourself, "I shoulda, coulda, woulda...?"

First of all, if you didn't do that action then, it was not the right time. Had you done "it," many of the great things in your current life may not exist today. For example, I believe I could have played professional baseball. I am certain that had I applied myself, I too, like a classmate, would have been drafted to the MLB to play baseball. This may sound great, but then I likely would not have learned the lessons I did, and this book would not be written in the context it is today. I would not have my three amazing children or my loving wife, René.

Wishing that you did something else in the past can be destructive thinking. Life is a journey of many roads and many seasons; opportunities are life's way of giving you the lessons you need to reach the places you are intended to be at each moment in time. How often have you been presented with an opportunity that repeats itself, but you acted on it days, weeks, or months later? The lessons and goals you reached were a sort of destiny, unique to you.

We have opportunities almost every day. An opportunity is really a chance to *do* something. To best describe what an opportunity is, let's use a sales analogy. Pretend you sell cars, and a couple walks in ready to buy a car. That couple offers you an *opportunity* to sell them a car. Here's another analogy: When you enroll in school and you read the list of classes you can choose from, you have the *opportunity* to choose your educational path.

Opportunities can become advantages; moreover, opportunities are advantages that should be "taken advantage of." Advantages, by themselves, are the result of our influence. I once had an opportunity to make a presentation to a very large hospital in Denver, Colorado. My company was competing for a large Medical Information Systems integration project that would require a lot of technical and organizational change scope work. The chief information officer (CIO) of the hospital decided to interview the four remaining competing companies as a group.

We all knew about this group interview, but we did not know who we would be competing against. My company had been working with this hospital for a couple of years, but our involvement was limited to single issues that were reactive, not proactive. This new project was a long-term strategic initiative that would require resources and even more technical and organizational skills than our company currently provided; however, we were uniquely qualified to expand our influence with this client.

When I walked into the group interview session, I immediately knew we were the underdog. Our firm was by far the smallest of the group, one-third to one-tenth the size of the companies we were competing against. I also knew each of the other companies very well.

The opportunity of the interview changed when I was afforded the advantage of presenting last. The benefit of going last is what turned this opportunity into an advantage. Each company had a stellar record of achievement when it came to the scope of work we were being asked to perform. As I sat there listening, I knew that I would need to make myself an orange in a basket full of apples; I needed to capitalize on my advantage of going last.

My opportunity to present my company began with the same background discussion everyone else used. I could see the eyes of the client's team begin to glaze over as I droned on about why my company should be chosen. At that point, one of the client's team members came right out and said to me, "Brian, your company is smaller than all of your competitors. Why should we choose your team over theirs?"

Advantage is a funny thing, and using your advantages properly is often an opportunity in and of itself. That one question from the client established how I was going to use my advantage of going last effectively. I looked at my client and then my competitors and answered, "Because my team has trained most of the people on their teams on how to do this project properly. Do you want the students, or do you want the teachers?"

You see, we had a training center that trained consultants from around the world. We had a tagline at the time: *Our Trainers Consult and Our Consultants Train.* To work for our company as a consultant meant that you also worked for us as a trainer, and we literally trained a good segment of the market competitors in the services needed by this client. This story provides an example of how remaining focused on the present moment can offer abundant opportunities, should you understand how to properly use your advantages.

Reading this book will show you how to create individual opportunities and how to turn those opportunities into viable results for you and those you influence. You will also learn why having a complete understanding of the (I)individual advantages that impact your life will help you and others to be better now and in the future.

To truly see all your individual advantages, you must realize that, in all success, you are not alone. Nobody on this earth can claim they are successful on their own, although we each play a key role in our own success. Some people call this being humble. I prefer to call it the realization that our significance was, in part, created by other individuals who substantially influenced us. There are still leaders and followers, primary roles and supporting roles. But each is important, and forgetting about those who got us to where we are in our journey devalues our individual advantage to ourselves and others.

Individual advantage, as you will see, is about self. It is about image. It is about others. It is about influence. It is about prosperity. It is about acceptance. It is about structure. It is about accountability, and it is about teamwork. This book is the foundation of what I have been applying and teaching people for over three decades. I have raised a family on these principles—a family secure in who they are and where they are in life. I have shared this way of life with my wife René for over 30 years. I have helped to build more than 50 companies, as well as assisted thousands of individuals to realize their advantages with our company, IA Business Advisors. Should you choose to be open, want to learn, and apply yourself—you will gain valuable insights that increase your strengths and influence using our philosophies. Should you continue reading, gaining the knowledge of your individual advantages will be invaluable.

Key Takeaways: Opportunities vs. Advantages

- Opportunities are life's way of giving us the information we need to reach the places at which we intend to arrive.

- Not all opportunities are intentional; many are created through the advantages we create as (I)individuals.

- If advantages are used properly, (I)individuals may find more abundant opportunities.

- Not recognizing the (I)individuals who have influenced you on your journey devalues some of your advantages and can affect your opportunities.

CHAPTER 2

SLOW DOWN

"Wisely, and slow.
They stumble
that run fast."
—William
Shakespeare

To begin this journey, we must slow down. Although there is no magic formula, and it may be difficult, one of the single most valuable pieces of advice I give to people on a daily basis is to slow down. Slowing down is a cornerstone of the foundation of understanding yourself. In order to look at what has made you who you are, you need to have patience, purpose, and a present, open mind.

Fast living manifests itself in many ways. Often when we say a person is living fast, we mean that their life is out of control by way of risk-taking. While it would be prudent for all of us to take stock of those parts of our lives where we may be living life too *large* (partying and other things that have potentially harmful consequences), I am writing about a different type of slowing down.

I used to live my life like a bull in a china shop. I used to charge into projects headlong. I'm that guy who buys a do-it-yourself furniture project and throws the instructions to the side, thinking that I can build the piece through some kind of absorbed or intuitive knowledge passed on to me by my parents at birth. The speed at which I got myself worked up was nothing less than amazing to those around me. As I began putting pieces together and finding myself more and more lost, I would direct my frustration and anger at the object itself because it was taking too long to build. Almost every time this would happen, René would say calmly, "Did you read the instructions?"

Who has time for that?!

I cannot tell you the number of times I spent twice the time struggling with a project that I would have if I had read the instructions in the first place. I was the stereotypical man who wouldn't ask for directions. I'm sure you know the type—the man who will drive in circles, insisting he knows how to get somewhere instead of stopping for a moment and asking for directions. Thank God for GPS.

For me, the lesson of slowing down did not take root until late 1999. In April 1999, we moved into our new home in Colorado. Our home was our first big purchase as a family; we built it as a celebration of our success. This home would also prove to be a catalyst for me to go warp speed, as it required me to perform even better as a professional and reach an imagined social status.

In October 1999, a friend and I stopped by the house during a workday, intending to have a cup of coffee before heading to a business meeting. As we talked in the kitchen, I went from cupboard to cupboard looking for the coffee cups, unable to find them. After about two or three cycles around the kitchen, I called out to René in a very frustrated tone, "Where are the damn coffee cups?!" The reply was classic René—with her blue eyes full of amusement and a smile spread across her freckled face, she opened the cupboard and did her best Vanna White as she showed me their very obvious location.

This story has lived on in our family as a humorous jab at my inability to slow down enough to locate the coffee cups in my own home after six months. It serves as a great lesson about people who are always preoccupied with what comes next. We have a tendency to race through life to get to some imaginary checkpoint that is generally created by us alone.

Thinking Forward

The first step in slowing down is acknowledging our tendency to go through life too fast. Have you ever heard someone say, "Whoa, pump the brakes and slow down a little"? I wish it were that simple but we are not cars, after all. I could have easily told that same thing to my kids when they came running up in a fervor of emotion and a jumble of words, facing an immediate crisis that, they felt, demanded my immediate attention. My first comment to my son or daughter, as they tugged at my hand or sleeve, attempting to drag me to the scene of the crisis, was always, "Slow down."

The most humorous part of this series of events is that I would say this to my children and then return to my own fast-paced thought process, where my mind was already two steps ahead. Or better yet, I'd find that I could not remember what I was doing and turn instead to some other immediate need.

However, the coffee cup incident was not my defining moment; I did not learn from my mistake. In fact, it's not even the most interesting example I have of me going too fast. The event that defines me going too fast as a professional, which I use day in and day out as an example, is what I like to call "Peanut Butter Syndrome."

The following story illustrates how the mind can take over when we are going too fast. The irony is not lost on me that peanut butter is in the story, a food that inherently slows you down with its gooey goodness.

One morning, I was in my typical rush (this won't be the last time you hear about my morning rushes!), and I was preparing for a big meeting with one of our clients on the south side of Denver. At the time, this client was our largest, and the project was very high-profile. We were designing an order entry system for a manufacturing company with offices located in three states. The project included computer programming work and business process re-engineering, as we were to integrate the system into the company's ERP (Enterprise Resource Planning) and accounting systems for real-time data access from anywhere in the company. This is a typical issue for me as a professional. Like every other morning, I already had the client on my mind. I was thinking about what I would be doing in three or four hours, things our team would be doing at that same time, and what we would be doing over the next days, weeks, and months.

In my rush, I just wanted some peanut butter on toast and coffee. Easy enough, right? By this time I actually remembered where the coffee cups were but for the life of me I could not find the peanut butter. We had a food cupboard that went from the floor to about six-feet high like a small pantry, which we called "Little Safeway." I stood in front of this cupboard with my mind racing about some flow chart or a conversation, and my peanut butter wishes fell someplace in the back. My frustration at not finding the peanut butter and the distraction from my important thoughts about factories and data had me once again calling out to René to rescue me from my own mind. This time there was no Vanna White moment. It was more like a flash of red hair and long arms reaching over my shoulder to grab the jar of peanut butter I was staring right in the face. With a chuckle and snort about not seeing something right in front of me, René handed me the peanut butter.

How many peanut butter moments does it take before you realize the speed of your mind is in control of even the most simple and basic things you see or do, even something as simple as grabbing food from the cupboard? The peanut butter moment replaced the coffee cup moment very quickly as René brought it up in jest. For me, this was a defining moment, a keen reminder of how life can be too fast and how we can lose sight of what is right in front of us.

You may be asking, "But how do I actually slow down?" In fact, this is a very complex question because, like all things, it needs to be put into context. My Peanut Butter Syndrome affected the speed at which I operated within the confines of my own home; however, going too fast affects everyone differently and produces various defining moments—each with a different remedy.

To best answer this question, I tell my own stories and give advice on what I have learned. In the context of your personal environment (home, family, vacation, friends, etc.), I recommend that you begin to remove work-related issues when you spend time there. For example, create a single space in your home where you are able to work, and don't allow yourself to be distracted with work issues anywhere else. This exercise itself will slow you down. When you remove work from your personal environment, you will notice your attention increase in your personal spaces. I used to work in my bedroom, kitchen, family room, garage—basically anywhere I had my phone—but now I have a specific workspace at home. The new rule at home is no work from my phone, tablet, or any document anywhere in the house except my workspace. I don't even answer the phone now at home; if it rings, I may physically disconnect from the personal things I am doing and walk into my workspace to review my calls. I defer even this to set working hours.

There are exceptions to all things, but I urge you not to make exceptions to any rule you establish until that rule has become a new *habit*. If you allow a call "just this once," it will lead to "just this second time," and ultimately, complete abandonment of the goal. Just as I am sure of this, I am also sure that your engagement with those around you, previously affected by your disassociation of your personal life in support of your fast-paced work life, will be positively influenced.

I will also mention some other personal areas that really do fall within the context of my peanut butter story. When with friends, put your phone away. If you have children, give them a special ringtone and keep your phone on, but ignore any ring that is not from them. When on vacation, set aside specific times, if any, when you will address work issues. For me, I wake up before René and the kids and log in to my email and get my work done before they wake up. Waking up early is a small sacrifice to have 100 percent engagement with my wife and kids on vacation. In support of these actions, establish expectations with your team, employer, clients, or anyone under your influence who may think they are more important than the time you are spending with family during a well-deserved vacation.

Oh, and if you're thinking to yourself, "It's easier said than done," I've heard that one a thousand times as well. Look, if you have people in your life who cannot live without your absence from a work environment for five to ten business days, you have allowed an unhealthy reliance on you among those who do not understand what your vacation means.

Today, I know the location of every coffee cup and the peanut butter in my home. I also know what my family is up to, and if I don't, it's generally because they are caught up in their own fast-paced issues. Compartmentalization of your time and workplace has tremendous benefits. Try it out—I dare you!

Key Takeaways: Thinking Forward

- When your mind becomes lost in thought, whether it be stuck in the future, past, or a distracting moment, it will take you away from and disrupt your present focus.

- Just as you do not bring your personal life to work, don't bring your work home unless you have designated a space for it.

- Do not make exceptions to the rule until you have established the habit. If you do make an exception, find value in it and recognize it is a one-time act and not the new normal.

- Set separate ringtones for those who are important to you or place them on your phone's favorites list to help manage unwanted distractions.

- If working is necessary while on vacation, establish a schedule with your family and your team to ensure your work/life balance meets everyone's expectations.

Environmental Urgency

Environmental urgency is when external factors influence you to feel as if you must go faster, perform better, and do more all around. Urgency doesn't solely exist at home, during your personal time. It can exist anywhere. You may even find that it is most prevalent in the workplace. While you work on the speed of your environment in your own home, it may be worthwhile to work on the speed of your environment at work, too, so that something as ludicrous as the following scenario does not happen to you.

Have you ever missed a meeting? Not: have you ever arrived late, or have you ever forgotten to call someone? I mean, have you utterly blown off a meeting with someone? I have.

I once served as a professional witness for a client's legal case. The client had nothing to do with any other business IA was involved in; our entire engagement was just to write a report. This client also had a skill that I saw as advantageous for more than a few of our other clients. His expertise was as a connector, as we like to call it—he had developed relationships around the world and, therefore, could connect people. Due to the sensitivity of providing the report for this client's case, both this gentleman and I went above and beyond to ensure that, should we have any discussions regarding other areas of business, it would not have a negative effect on this case or cause any other conflict of interest. Both of us had discussions with attorneys and our teams in an effort to prepare for the opportunity to meet.

On the day of our meeting, I was excited about the possibility of having an asset that could solve a long-standing issue we were facing at IA. That morning, I met with a couple of my team members to go over my later meeting with this client; we were doing our last-minute due diligence. My entire day was built around this meeting (knowing that the lunch spot we had decided on was 30 minutes from my office). Around 9:45 a.m., I was hit with a number of pressing client issues. These issues seemed to be fueled by their inability to slow down.

As you can surmise, I worked right through my meeting time and well into the next hour. My phone was on silent, my email alerts were turned off, and my door was shut, allowing me to deeply focus on the work at hand. I was brought out of this deep thought by a knock at my door and one of our team members asking me, "Weren't you supposed to meet Mr. So-and-so for lunch today?"

It was an hour and ten minutes past my meeting time, meaning it was an hour and forty minutes past the time I was supposed to leave. My client, a gracious and rather calm individual, coincidentally also spent the time at our proposed meeting point working on other projects. He did not notice that it was well past the original agreed-upon time.

Do I miss a lot of meetings? No. Am I late for meetings? Yes. The issue of going too fast almost always creates delays. The domino effect of missing this meeting with my client caused a month-long delay in manufacturing, operations, and other areas of business for us both. We both have busy schedules, not just locally but internationally. Setting aside time to meet was already difficult, and the discussions we needed to have required us to be face-to-face. The act of going too fast and missing our original meeting meant we missed opportunities to connect with other parties as well.

Even though each of us woke up that morning with specific goals related to each other and projected those thoughts and goals into our morning routine, we still allowed the urgency of our environment to distract us. While some may say this is an exception or a personal character flaw, 30 years of working with professionals and supporting teams have shown me that this is the norm. Speed of action and speed of thought, in most environments, causes mistakes that ultimately cause delays. Ironic, isn't it?

Earlier I noted that not all types of going too fast are the same, and that each requires a different remediation. My goal is to give you tools for how to avoid each type of "going too fast" moment. When you are going fast to the point where you completely forget something or miss a deadline, you are distracted by your immediate environmental urgencies. Our goal is to challenge, and ultimately change, this bad habit.

First, when you have an important meeting or deadline, have someone (whether it be a friend, family, or team member) hold you accountable. Outside accountability will help you to slow down and serve as a reminder on days that you are deeply embedded in other things. (Having someone hold you accountable will also help you create a habit and may combat some of the difficulties that we all face in slowing down.) Another benefit of allowing a third party to offer you accountability is that it will help you practice identifying your tasks specific to that day's work.

Having a third party assist with accountability may seem like an unusual task, but for many of us, technology does not work as a reminder. We have become so used to the noise created by technology it often fails as our source of accountability. However, having someone in your office, or your spouse, or a close friend support you in changing a habit that will benefit you for the rest of your life is not a lot to ask.

In my case, I ask René to text me or call me to remind me of important personal things. She is my first line of defense and serves to add one extra mental marker. Over time, I have been able to rely on this tactic less because I have built up the habit of listening to my technological reminders. In the past, I would have easily forgotten these tasks. My new habits have spread into other areas of my life, and I have been able to improve my memory altogether through the act of outsourced accountability.

When I am at work, I rely on my team or peers for this accountability. I am open with my team about my ability to recall information or stick to specific schedules. I work with them regularly to ensure that I stay on track individually, and Individually we continue to progress.

This accountability oversight does not need to last forever. Some may say that this tactic will result in total reliance on others for accountability. However, that is actually the exception, not the rule. When you work proactively to rectify a proficiency, you create a moment and habit of slowing down to create your own mental marker. What generally happens is that when you have something important coming up, you are able to remember it before a third party holds you accountable, thus creating a new and healthy habit.

The second trick I would recommend is to NOT turn off your cellphone. Sometimes turning your cell phone off is useful when you need to focus on one thing, but when you are planning a big event, it may be helpful to keep your cell phone on in case anyone calls to remind you (accountability!). When you get in the habit of listening to your phone for reminders, you can set those reminders and alarms on your phone. There are tons of reminder and alarm apps for your phone and computer that can aid in keeping you on track for your day. They are truly helpful when you are able to break the habit of ignoring them.

Key Takeaways: Environmental Urgency

- Speed of action and speed of thought, in most environments, cause mistakes that may ultimately cause delays.

- Are you often late or missing meetings? If you have an important meeting or deadline, ask someone to hold you accountable. This request doesn't need to last forever. Have someone hold you accountable until you feel secure and have created a habit of slowing down.

- On days when you have important deadlines or meetings, do not silence or turn off your phone; use it to create reminders of those events you need to focus on.

Subconscious Mode

Going too fast can also manifest itself in our personal lives. I have a few hobbies, none of which require my focus for a long time. For example, I collect stamps. At certain times, I will focus on them and then put them away for years before I even think about them again. Similarly, I like coins, building models, puzzles, reading, knives, and video games. Like stamp collecting, I get into these hobbies for a while and then set them aside for a longer while.

One day, I was sitting in the garage with René and Henry, and I was messing with one of my knives. It happened to be one I inherited from my stepfather, Bill, when he passed away. At the time, Henry was about 8. I was managing IA globally, as well as a couple of very high-profile investments in southern Oregon: a hotel and a family entertainment center. My mind was very much in "subconscious mode" (a.k.a. autopilot) as I whittled a stick and contemplated issues at all three entities. Henry wanted to whittle a stick too, and he brought me one he found in the yard, with a request for me to show him how to do it in the only way an 8-year-old knows how: persistent begging.

Now, despite my position on slowing down and my experience teaching the value of it, Henry was interrupting important thoughts about clients, hotel rooms, and families at our entertainment center. So, to appease my son *and* to focus on all those immediate things on my mind, I allowed Henry to whittle. René was quick to point out how dangerous it might be for our 8-year-old boy to "play" with a knife… to which I replied, in haste, that I would teach him knife safety.

"Don't worry; I'm his dad."

The next few moments would slow down the rest of the day *and* the following week. In my desire to get back to thinking about client problems and hotel and restaurant operations, I cut off the tip of my finger teaching Henry about knife safety.

Cutting off the tip of my finger is a dramatic lesson in going too fast, and while it's not typical of what going too fast can cause in our day-to-day lives, the scar on my finger is my proverbial reminder to slow down. Most of us forget something, leave something unfinished, drop something, or complete tasks in haste on a regular basis because of our need to speed through to another quickly performed task.

Sometimes it takes extreme examples to get a point across and remind yourself to slow down. Going too fast manifests itself differently in each of our lives, and I hope that I never cut off another part of my body to remind myself to slow down.

Another symptom of going too fast can involve forgetting key requirements for our activities. René is always telling me to make lists. I travel extensively and have for many years. I get ready for each trip the night before I leave. I use a CPAP, but otherwise, I don't have any special toiletries for travel; I rely on memory to pack toiletries last. Depending on how fast I am going that morning, even though I have been packing the same way for over three decades, I will often forget something. Once I forgot my CPAP altogether and had to buy a new one when I landed.

If you find that you often forget silly little things, or even big things, this is a key indicator that you are going too fast. Your haste can manifest itself in other ways as well: maybe you leave things behind at work and have to backtrack; maybe you forget something in your car; maybe you miss calls or appointments, or maybe you lose track of time or words during conversations (possibly losing track of an entire conversation).

Another way going too fast can manifest itself is in the context of meetings or speaking engagements. If you end up speaking too fast, you may find that the person you are speaking to cannot keep up with this fast pace; they may not be able to directly follow your train of thought. If you find that you must repeat yourself often, maybe they can't hear you or aren't listening. However, it's more likely that you are going too fast. When speaking, we often don't consider that the person we are speaking to does not have the foundation of knowledge of the topic being discussed. We make this mistake often; we know what we want to say, but it doesn't always come out as clearly as we understand it in our heads. We can quickly digress in our own heads, taking turns in conversation without warning others. These turns in our thinking negatively impact the speed at which our audience can react.

Digression is often a key sign of going too fast; it's the way the speed of our mind manifests in our communication. In writing, you see this same type of issue. When you write too fast, it will manifest itself in what can only be called gibberish—in handwriting more so than in typing. When writing, we may quickly lose track of what we have written due to the lack of interaction with others because writing is a solely personal discussion. Our mind continues to speed along to the point that we can get lost in our thoughts— subconsciously typing or writing along—and we know the full story only in our mind. However, you may find that the words don't quite make sense to anyone else.

I cannot tell you how many times a team member has handed me back a paper and said, "What are you trying to say here?" when I understand it perfectly in my mind. Originally, I hand-wrote a good portion of this book in my Moleskine journal. Upon examination, the variation in my handwriting is bizarre. I must have close to ten different styles with one hand alone—and I'm ambidextrous. This is a clear manifestation of how fast my mind is going and what kind of headspace I am in while writing.

While conversation and interaction can slow the process of verbal communication down, leaving less room for errors and more room for dialogue should anyone become lost, written communication is another ballgame. With my team, I have to keep in mind that no one else understands the *context* of the issues I am writing about because there is no space for questions in writing.

As you can see from these examples, going too fast can manifest itself anytime and anywhere, and when it does, the best advice I have is to *slow down*. You will see improvements quickly and find that you are more efficient. It will take time and patience to benefit from the act of slowing down. If you are like most people I have encountered, you may even have some push-back to the act of slowing down.

What can be gained by slowing down and not rushing through tasks? You may say to yourself, "There is no way I can go any slower. There is not enough time in the day!" My initial reply is always the same: We all have the same amount of time in a day. The conversation always leads to the amount of work that "needs" to be completed in that same amount of time.

We can always come up with an excuse not to slow down. Our boss has demands. Customers have demands. Peers have demands. How about you, do you have demands? Self-reflection can be a big part of slowing down. Is ego causing you to push past your limits? Do you have an image of yourself and your work that propels you to move quickly, to impress others with your hard work and drive? What would happen if you slowed down to 90 percent of your current pace? What about 80 or even 70 percent? What situational awareness would you develop? How much more focus would you have? How much clearer would your own internal and external communication become?

Key Takeaways: Subconscious Mode

- Are you often forgetting one too many things? You're likely going too fast. Make a checklist to ensure nothing is forgotten—especially on your travels. Making lists is a good "slow down" exercise.

- When communicating, connect with your audience and consider their point of view by engaging in feedback on the topic. Try not to digress.

- If you choose the avenue of written communication, be mindful of reviewing your work. If it's handwritten, ensure that it's legible enough for others to read. Upon review, look for areas to edit with more or less information depending on your audience. Add context when discussing new topics with new people and provide only the necessary details when writing to those already in the know.

Immediate Gratification

Speed can result in miscommunication or negative communication. Time demands and the internal need to speed along can put nerves on edge and create environments where people tend to communicate less or in ways that are ineffective. We find ourselves reacting to another person's haste or impatience with negative judgments, often steering the discussion onto tangents that only feed negativity and provide nothing constructive to the original issue. Going too fast tests patience, and in today's world of need for immediate gratification—or I should say, of demands for information or action—a lack of patience often leads to disagreement.

I still struggle to find solutions to the need for immediate gratification. We are bombarded with a need to immediately react or complete tasks—sometimes consciously but more often subconsciously. One only has to walk down a street full of people to notice what today's technology has done to humans' need for speed.

When I travel, there is one universal action that is consistent in every town I visit: cell phone usage. Cell phones are no longer just a phone; they are also TVs, workspaces, computers, game consoles, and much more. Want to freak out a human between the ages of 13 and 50? Take away their cell phone.

With the applications available to us, we can manage most of our life on our cell phone—from communicating with people to turning on the lights in our homes. Want to know where your teenager is? Look it up on your phone. Missing your favorite TV show and don't want to wait? Get the Hopper™ by Dish and watch on your phone in real time.

These kinds of technologies have created the need for immediate gratification. Patience is waning in all aspects of human interaction, and the whole of society is affected. I identified this issue in my dissertation long before it became a commonly known problem: Technology Induced Attention Deficit Disorder (TIADD).

There are many places in society where this manifests itself on a regular basis. Let's begin with a prosaic example of immediate versus lasting gratification: cupcakes.

To eat a cupcake is to have immediate gratification. Most people enjoy cupcakes like Lay's Potato Chips: you can't eat just one. Those who eat cupcakes in search of immediate gratification of their need for sweets may be jeopardizing their potential long-term gratification of being fit and healthy. Individuals focusing on how they feel now often lose sight of the long-term consequences of a single but repetitive act. Eating just one cupcake occasionally is not bad, but the *habit* of eating several cupcakes has derailed many plans for a thin summer physique.

The internet is another place where humans have adapted to expect faster gratification. In 1995, when I began using the internet on a regular basis, I used AOL as my service provider. My first modem was a 14,400 baud rate modem that made crazy digital sounds and required me to use a phone line to connect. I would sit in front of my computer and wait patiently for it to download messages, photos, and website content, amazed at the amount of information I could access and work with on my computer.

In 1997, when I was designing ERP (Enterprise Resource Planning) systems around the world, I began working with 128,000 baud rate digital network connections that did not require a standard phone line. In two years, the speed at which we communicated over the internet had increased tenfold. The amount of data we could transfer and share also increased, allowing more people to access this data and allowing us to do more. The wait for messages, photos, and website content decreased tremendously.

By 2001, when I argued my dissertation on TIADD, I was still designing and implementing ERP systems and working with companies to manage the organizational change being caused by the influence of technology on humans. Internet access rates were increasing, and you could get a 128,000 baud rate at home and a 1,544,000 baud rate at work. In less than five years, we had again increased the speed of communication over tenfold. Humans quickly adapted to this increase and raised expectations for their data.

Through the years, from 2001 to now, we have seen data speeds increase more than fiftyfold. We have also expanded the influence of technology from the workplace, to home, to the back of your pocket. This transformation in data delivery has created an insistent need for immediate gratification of knowledge; we need answers *this instant.*

This need for immediate gratification has had a negative influence on human relationships in all aspects, from quality to quantity. In 1997, if we wanted the immediate gratification of speaking to someone, we picked up the phone, wrote a letter, or visited them personally. We took our time, and the conversations were thoughtful and memorable. How many visits or phone calls to people in your life do you remember?

During Christmas of 1990, I had just begun dating René. I already knew I was in love with her, and our first months of dating had been typical of the time. We talked on the phone and saw each other as often as we could. René and I had some "missed communications," which made me feel kind of insecure. So, while shopping for René at Aurora Mall in Colorado, I stopped at a payphone and called her. Our call lasted for almost an hour, and to this day is something we both remember. That hour-long phone call had meaning; it had context.

Today, we text. We talk about life and what is going on, but I cannot tell you anything meaningful that we discuss via text. Unlike that phone call over 30 years ago, texting is immediate and at such a speed that most of its content is lost as soon as we are interrupted with the next text, email, or other notification—it has far less meaning in the grand scheme of our lives.

There was a lot of long-term gratification in communication prior to advances in communication technology. Today, people post or tweet in order to immediately satisfy the need to say something to remain relevant. Almost gone are the days when we cut out a news article about a loved one or put a picture in a photo album to create a book where we sit around the table and look at things that once provided long-term gratification.

The propensity to quickly move from issue to issue and juggle texts from work, friends, and family—while we are also trying to perform manual tasks at work or home—diminishes the value of the information we receive. In our workplace, we often see gaps or mistakes caused by the interruptions that come from the amount of information being thrown at us. I am guilty of this myself, and sometimes to the detriment of my team. Brenda, who works with me on a daily basis, is seated right outside my office. She is responsible for work that requires great focus and detail; I know this, as does she. However, I often just yell out to her and interrupt whatever she is doing to satisfy my own immediate need. If I'm not in my office and want a similar response, I text her and skip email—knowing that she will respond more quickly to a text.

My need for immediate gratification may resolve the issue at hand but it allows interruptions to invade the current chosen task or me or those I influence. These interruptions create risks that either my work or the work of the person I am interrupting will not be completed to the best of our abilities. Focus requires us to find a way to keep ourselves and our influence in sync for our personal and team objectives. The best way to do this is to create a *deliberate* environment.

Key Takeaways: Immediate Gratification

- Speed can result in miscommunication and/or negative communication. We often know what is in our minds, so we may pass over details when communicating. We also don't usually know how much knowledge another individual has on the subject, but we may assume.

- When possible, slow down and have thoughtful and meaningful conversations.

- Be mindful of the communications you send out using technology. It's easy to quickly say something you might regret.

- When technology slows down, freezes, or leaves you with an infinite loading circle, remind yourself to have patience; technology has come a long way.

Slow Down Reflection

Slowing down may be the most important aspect of your journey to aid in your discovery of self. Without slowing down, you are unable to organize thoughts and emotions and remain present. These are key to discovering your foundation and learning more about what makes you *you*. As you continue on your path, slow down, and come into the present, you will find that these actions inherently cause you to focus. Use this focus to keep you on your path of discovery.

CHAPTER 3

Focus

"What you stay
focused on
will grow."
—Roy T. Bennett

Focus is a byproduct of slowing down, and one of the best ways to gain that focus is by being in the present moment. When you are in the present moment, you are wholly focused. Centering yourself allows your mind to enter a state of calm that allows you to retrieve memories, logically ponder your life's events, respond to stimuli in your current environment, and more. What is of extreme importance is that we understand that our ability to influence or be influenced requires us to be our best in the present moment, and the only way to achieve that is to have focus.

Most of us know that focus is required to be our best self. However, staying in the present moment can be difficult.

Deliberate Acts

As I alluded to earlier, there is but one overarching way to slow down: being deliberate. Being deliberate requires discipline and focus, but once you develop the habit of deliberate action, the world around you will slow down to a pace where focus becomes your first byproduct. There is always a way to be deliberate in all we do. I will use face-to-face communication as my example here.

When speaking to someone, either one-on-one or in a group, how many times do you allow for distraction? I'm not sure any of us can be involved in a conversation nowadays without being distracted by our cell phones. One of the rules implemented at IA is that cell phones are not allowed out in the open when dealing with a client. It is imperative that each member of our team is deliberate with the time they give to our clients. Too often, we are communicating with someone and they look down at their phone, distracting themselves, undermining the integrity of our discussion.

Not being distracted by a phone is a deliberate act to focus on the conversation you are having. This is not a difficult deliberate act to begin with, and it will slow you down and direct your attention on the matter at hand: the conversation.

The second deliberate act you can have during in-person communication is to look at the person speaking. Physically looking at the person will help you focus on their words and not daydream or digress in your own mind about some other task or issue that is not currently relevant. Looking someone in the eye conveys something to those you are communicating with and, in turn, to you: respect. Often, one of the first compliments I get about my children is that they look people in the eye when speaking to others. My children have learned to focus on those who speak and to show their respect. This kind of respect will earn you the same in return.

The act of paying attention by removing distractions and looking at those who are speaking will slow down the rate at which your mind accepts the communication you are receiving. Your mind is not trying to listen to someone across the room at the same time you read a text message or email from someone else, which then forces you to focus on a reply, emotion, or feeling based on the information you are reading. Pretty soon, you have missed a sentence, paragraph, or more from the person speaking. This is a common issue with multi-tasking, the ultimate form of going too fast. When you slow down how your mind processes information, you become more efficient *and* act as a positive influence.

Key Takeaways: Deliberate Acts of Focus

- Being deliberate in your thoughts and actions is one great way to slow down and remain in the present.

- Not allowing yourself to be distracted by a phone is a deliberate act of focus on the task you are engaged in.

- Looking at the person with whom you are speaking is a deliberate act of focus that benefits you and the other party.

Comfortable Focus

Another type of going too fast is what I like to call "comfortable focus." In this state, we become so accustomed to what we are doing that we no longer think about the *act* of what we do and just go through the motions. Comfortable focus is being so confident with what we do that our mind wanders while our subconscious and physical self completes tasks. (Other terms for this are "autopilot" and "muscle memory.") Some may see this as a form of multitasking; however, I see it as allowing the world to pass by, right along with opportunity and advantage.

The best analogy I have for this involves driving. Driving is one area of our lives where we can often go too fast. I'm not necessarily talking about how fast we drive, but how many thoughts and distractions we have while doing it. When we moved to Oregon and then later to Illinois, I had relatively short commutes to my offices: two miles in Oregon and eight miles in Illinois. The path to the office, in both cases, was pretty simple; not a lot of turns and stops, meaning that I could get into a routine and drive the route with a comfortable focus. One day, while driving to work in Oregon, I looked up and saw a house I had never noticed, after three months of the same daily drive. Why did I notice that house after three months? I had to slow down due to construction and actually pay attention to what I was doing.

Going through the motions and being comfortable with our surroundings or people can lull us into a false sense of security. The National Highway Traffic Safety Administration reports that approximately 52 percent of all accidents occur within a 5-mile radius of home, and 69 percent of all car accidents occur within a 10-mile radius from home.[1] This false sense of security leads people to think that talking on their cell phones, eating, and getting lost in their music while driving is safe since they have muscle memory for the roads. While knowing the roads closest to your home is appropriate, you also need to be prepared for the child who darts into the street chasing after a ball or the reckless driver who is also in a comfortable focus and may not see you.

Getting into our cars is a form of emotional and psychological comfort and security. Most of us feel comfortable enough not to think about the action of driving. However, that feeling can stretch beyond the drive. The more we repeat something, the more of a habit it becomes, and the higher chance we will take our actions for granted. During this time we can speed up our minds and allow ourselves to be arrogant about our ability to complete certain tasks. You may be saying to yourself, "Driving to work and not recognizing a building or sign has no real effect on my life." While this

1. (2008) "Many Car Accidents Occur Close to Home" Pines Salomon Injury Lawyers, APC. https://seriousaccidents.com/blog/many-car-accidents-occur-close-to-home/. Accessed 22 Feb 2018

may generally be true, the process of comfortable focus can get to a point where important things get missed, as my next story of an atypical morning will reveal.

My mornings are generally as structured as my drive; I am typically in a comfortable focus for most of it. The only thing that varies is the clothes I wear; "to wear a suit or to not wear a suit" is the constant variable in my morning routine. This particular day, I had to wear a suit. It was not an ordinary day. I rushed to get ready for work as my mind was overly occupied with a meeting I was about to have at a big hospital on the south side of Denver. This meeting was going to be different; my company could become the hospital's consulting partner in the development of a new medical records management system, and we were the new kids on the playground. Needless to say, I was playing out my presentation in my mind.

It was an early summer morning, so René and the kids were still asleep. I put on my sports jacket, slipped on my wingtip shoes, and double-tied them as I always do. I blew through coffee and breakfast, which was not typical of me at this time in my life; I usually enjoyed my mornings at home. We lived on a golf course and our backyard was adjacent to the fifth tee box. We also had a lake and another whole fairway for hole four behind us, not to mention a complete, unobstructed view of the Flatirons and the Rocky Mountains. On this day, the striking view was lost on me because my brain was thinking forward.

However, when preparing for work, I know how I prepare best. I don't procrastinate in the sense that I put things off subconsciously. I put things off to a point where the demand to get them done gives me added focus and drive; now who's fooling who, right? Comfortable focus helps me here in the mornings. I don't really need to think about getting dressed, making coffee, driving to work; I can do most of that in my sleep.

With my mind racing at full speed, the act of preparing my physical self was in comfortable focus. (By the way, I am also a car guy.) It was a nice day out, a little cool as Colorado mornings can be, but otherwise a beautiful summer morning. Our home in Colorado had a tandem three-car garage, meaning that on this day, I was going to have to move one car to get to the one I wanted to drive. My mind was skipping from bullet point to bullet point about our proposed solutions to the hospital and our plan to be better than companies a hundred times our size and eons older. I went through the routine of moving cars and putting the top down on the one I was going to drive.

Ready to leave, I made one last round of checks in my home, which I still do today. I look to make sure I have put my coffee cup in the sink. I say goodbye to everyone in my home, even guests; this habit is so ingrained that to have closure on my morning, I won't miss a single person. I will look over my tools of the trade, my briefcase or computer bag, to ensure that I have everything I need for the day. I rarely forget anything at home.

After I determined I was ready, I hopped into my car, now sitting outside in front of the garage. We lived in a quiet area north of Denver with little early-morning traffic. As I pulled onto I-25 South, I got a chance to put my car through some high-rev acceleration and quickly got up to 70 to 80 miles per hour, all while keeping my mind focused on work.

Close to I-76—about 13 miles into my drive, where the highway becomes congested—my mind snapped out of its comfortable focus of work and onto the road. This day, however, I noticed more of a breeze than normal. I had indeed missed something that I could not give my presentation without: my pants.

Somehow, I had managed to get through my entire morning of comfortable focus with no pants. My habits were so ingrained and automatic that I even double-tied my shoes with bare legs.

Our minds can do things that defy simple logic. Noticing whether or not I had pants on should be pretty logical. Putting on my suit coat, tie, and shoes should have been enough for my mind to notice something this obvious. Walking around, getting in and out of cars as I moved them, and leaving one outside running while I put one back to then go back into the house to do my goodbyes and check for all my tools of the trade—you'd think I'd recognize even the slightest difference. However, my comfortable focus with my routine of the day, coupled with my speed of thought, was powerful enough to allow me to drive 13 miles down the highway without slowing my mind down. My focus was broken by one thing: traffic.

I began consciously thinking about living in the present about the same time I drove off with no pants. In fact, I drove back to my house without noticing anything other than how I could have walked out the door without pants.

Key Takeaways: Comfortable Focus

- The more we repeat something, and the more of a habit it becomes, the higher the chance we will begin taking our actions for granted by engaging in comfortable focus (auto-pilot).

- Leaving your home without pants is a good indication your mind is elsewhere.

Living in the Present

After the no-pants situation, I realized that I needed to be present to understand 100 percent of what was happening. Living in the present is a form of slowing down. I immediately equated traffic on the highway with the issue that caused me to walk out the door without pants; traffic makes you come back to reality, back to the present. Traffic forces you to focus on the cars in front of you, to both sides, and maybe even behind you. Traffic makes you slow down and pay attention.

Being present is a conscious effort. The trap of comfortable focus can overtake us before we know it and last until something snaps us out of our trance. Being present is something that we can learn, just like learning to walk. And for many of us, it will be just as difficult.

In the morning, I set myself up to be present throughout my day. I create reminders and alarms on my phone and notifications on my Outlook calendar. Luckily, these simple tools are available to us all. Over time, I have developed the habit of listening to these tools to break my comfortable focus and bring me back to the present. For example, I have hard deadlines for reviewing certain reports that are required before people are paid on an agreed-upon day. I remind myself to work out, write, or take vitamins. When we are busy, even the most simple distraction can upset things we think are habitual. One thing that is very difficult to ignore is a buzzer, timer, or tool intended to disrupt your current train of thought, such as the alarms attached to my phone and calendar.

Being in tune with our chosen methods of remembering things requires some work and the action/habit of actually listening to our reminders. Countless times I have slept through or worked through my reminders; I had to train myself to develop the habit of responding to these tools. One word of caution: do not allow yourself to ignore these tools, or the act of ignoring them will become part of your comfortable focus, and they will be ineffective.

The mind itself is such a powerful tool. We can use our brain's power to our advantage; we only need to work the parts that will support our desire to be in the present. We need to train our minds to acknowledge our outside triggers—or, I should say, to resist letting our mind take us from thought to thought and action to action while in comfortable focus. To do this, we need habit and willpower.

Later in this book, I will expand upon habit and willpower and the influence they both have on our ability to be our best for ourselves and others. Our own influence on others is affected and can be limited by our habits and willpower.

When you begin to train your mind to acknowledge your outside triggers in order to remove yourself from a comfortable focus, this can often feel like a disruption and may evoke negative emotions. Negative emotions can occur due to several factors, predominantly because being pulled from our world into the present doesn't always feel good; it can be a jolt that can shock the mind, in turn creating some negative feelings toward the disruption. However, effectively getting into the present moment includes being able to control these negative emotions. Being so focused on work that we are almost in a trance means that unexpected distractions can be quite upsetting. Each distraction brings us back to the present, which often means pulling us away from one of many places we were in our minds. This is where data can be lost, too.

I often find myself in my office working on tasks only to recognize that my mind is wandering to other areas of responsibility before that set-aside time. I may be waiting for a call, have unfinished tasks from the past, or have learned some new information about a project. These distractions from my present task are easy for me to control now; I simply write them down on a pad of paper. Putting them to paper slows down my mind enough to get me back to the task at hand.

However, there are times when an interruption will make me lose track of the work I was trying to get done. At that moment, I may stop everything in an attempt to get my bearings back and stare at my desk while my mind restores the right visuals in my head. These distractions raise the emotional frustration I feel. My frustration is led by two issues. One, I cannot believe that I am unable to remember what I was thinking about twenty seconds prior. Two, I am not happy with the person who interrupted me or the reason I was interrupted.

I have created some rules in support of keeping me in the present. (I help to hold myself accountable!) One rule that I have shared with everyone in our office is that walking in and distracting me when I am obviously focused on a task could elicit a brief negative response as I transition from my comfortable focus back to the present moment and their needs. If I really need to focus, meaning that I need deep-mind-work time where my present moment is *intended* to be comfortable focus on a specific topic, I close my door and turn off my phones. I also ask people to notify me if I think particular work may take me into that trance state. When you need to concentrate, comfortable focus can be a positive and necessary state.

Living in the present is not about being available to all the chaos around you. It's about having situation awareness and controlling your present focus. Comfortable focus is necessary at times; we all need time to lose ourselves in our own minds, work, or hobby. But we still need something that can bring us back to our overall present awareness and allow us to function without missing life as it goes by.

The things I do to keep one foot in the present include setting up distractions in my environment that force me to take note of the present: task reminders, visual cues within the documents I am working on, sticky notes, or (as I have mentioned previously) having a peer interrupt me at a specific time. These planned distractions can serve as a breather and allow you to check preplanned schedules, agendas, or other organizational tracking tools to ensure that you are meeting your own timelines for the tasks you want to complete.

One note about implementing planned distractions: you will find that if you previously reacted poorly to a distraction, you will continue to do so—at first. The habit of going into deep concentration and losing track of time, and then coming out of that in a foul mood, are two separate issues. While I don't generally like working on multiple habits so closely connected, these two require some collaboration. Be honest and upfront about your reactions and consciously remind yourself internally or with other visual cues, as we have discussed, that being present is a goal. For example, one of the cues I put up is "Don't get angry with disruption!" This cue and others are on sticky notes around my office, workbooks, and computers to remind me to be nice.

Key Takeaways: Living in the Present

- Being present is something that you can learn. Just like learning to walk, it will likely be difficult. But you must slow down and focus to create a habit of being present.

- Your mind is a powerful tool, and you're in control. You are responsible for your influence.

- If your mind is distracting you from present tasks, write your thoughts down to get them out. Keep a notebook or digital note for your thoughts. This will help you reflect on them and use them for positive influence.

Intentions

One of the best ways to slow down is to be intentional in all we do. Setting intentions is making a plan for how to think and act in advance. It is a mental state that prepares us to follow through on our commitments. In order to be intentional, we need to be focused. And to be focused, we need to slow down. If it is your intention to have patience, what must you do *today* to aid in achieving that patience? Does this include meditation? Time alone? What actions will you take to accomplish your intentions?

The difference between a goal and an intention is that goals can feel abstract, while intention is linked more directly with the actions needed to reach those goals. Goals are abstract because they are rooted in the future, while intentions are focused on the present moment. Your goals have a concrete beginning and end, while you should live out your intentions each and every day. Lastly, your goals can be seen and measured by others. Your intentions are personal, so they are part of your internal self-communication.

Deceleration of your fast-paced life can begin with the process of setting your daily intention. For me, I carve out 15 to 30 minutes of my morning and set my intention for the day. This action of setting aside the time was, in fact, an act of intention itself, to help me reach my ultimate goal of slowing down my entire life. Through the initial act of looking at my day ahead, I reinforce a number of intentions in my life.

Here are some intentions that are influenced by my initial act of setting my daily intention:

1. Make sure that I am the most important person in my life and that I am living to my fullest potential, to benefit me and those I influence.

2. Take responsibility for myself, reflect on my overall goals, and remind myself to remain focused on the present and slow down.

3. Remember that others influence me and that their influence is part of why I am successful.

4. Be prepared for my day with a clear understanding of my scheduled responsibilities.

5. Remain educated and relevant in industries I influence through my coaching, advising, and consulting.

6. Reinforce my team by understanding any issues they are facing and asking me for support on.

These are six high-level intentions that I set for myself, which lay the foundation for me to succeed personally and professionally. I also believe that these intentions, when reaffirmed on a daily basis, create in me the ability to remain present and slow down to ensure that my influence is objective, clear, and with purpose. I have paraphrased my intentions and reinforce them visually by writing them in my daily planner. "Remain Educated and Relevant" is a common scribble. "Be Prepared for Your Day" is another.

Each morning I read what I call "trade rags." My use of trade rags, or trade magazines, blogs, and newsletters, is a way I have remained educated and relevant for years. I advise my clients to utilize them to stay up-to-date on what is going on. One can garner vast knowledge from industry publications that you would not learn in five years of operations. People who share their experience and knowledge through print compound our knowledge and make us more intuitive in the areas we wish to start or continue learning about.

My intention to read about my areas of influence is fueled by my passion to be the best I can as a consultant, leader, peer, and person. Connecting your personal goals to your intentions will help to reinforce your goals and make your intentions more available to your present self. Without motivation, the act of being intentional can be lost in the chaos and clutter of your life. Your intention to change, learn, act, speak, or listen can be missed and then lost. Intentions are the seeds of action, similar in this way to goals.

When we are intentional, we immediately slow down. Setting your intentions provides the focus that you need to achieve them. When you set your intention, you should get in the habit of limiting outside interference: email, text, people, and so on. My recommendation is that you do this in a closed, private room. You may find that during this time, other thoughts will pop into your head that are not related. Keep a paper and pen close at hand so that you may write these thoughts down and refocus your attention on your intentions. For example, I often find myself working on a project when something triggers my mind about another issue I need to deal with. When this happens, I sometimes pivot to that new issue and lose focus on my current one; I lose my intention to remain focused on the present moment. My office is littered with the notes I write to myself during these times.

Whatever way you choose to keep your focus, make time to be intentional about your thoughts. I would suggest planning a separate time to focus on your new notes and turn them into something you can act upon. It boils down to this: You must become determined to *manage* your intentions. For some, this will be a simple task; for others, it will require practice.

Strive to make setting your intentions a habit. Creating habits in support of action to slow you down and keep you focused on your influences will be some of the best personal work you can do. Later in this book, we will look at how to reinforce your personal goals and amplify your ability to be successful in your quest to meet those goals.

Gaining focus also encompasses overall time management. Setting your time for being intentional will not work if you don't gain control over all of the time in your life. Developing habits that reinforce positive intentions is good. In the next section, we'll look at time from a different perspective.

Key Takeaways: Intention

- One of the best ways to slow down is to become intentional in all you do. To be intentional is to focus on the task at hand; try to build habits that keep you in the moment.

- Without motivation to guide your intention, the act of being intentional can be lost in the chaos and clutter of your life. You must *want* to be present. The act of being present is the beginning of intention, and the act of *staying* present is the reward for that intention.

Time Flies by So Quickly

Does time have to fly by? When I hear parents say, "Wow, kids grow up fast," I can't help but think, *Really? A day is a day. You must have been distracted by life.* The less present and the more distracted you are, the faster time will appear to go by because your perception of that time is different. Regardless of how slow or fast time seems to move, we all share the same *amount* of time. It is always moving at the same speed, in one direction. What changes is not time but only the perception of that time. What we as humans do with this gift is our biggest advantage. So, I ask you: What do you do with your time?

Time has not always been measured as it is today. Until the 19th century, there were no standard time zones adjusted by location on Earth. By this I mean that the current time differed from city to city, even within the same region; in one city, it could be 12:40 p.m., but in the next city, it might be 1:20 p.m. according to the town clock tower. At that time in England, however, railroads were becoming more popular. People relied on trains to move people and materials, and the relative time of each city was becoming an issue. England decided to standardize time based on the meridians of the world. In 1884, the adaptation of time zones began to catch on, and now we have standard time zones around the world.

What do time zones have to do with time flying by? Perception. Soon after the development of synchronized time, the world began to look at time differently. We began to measure time against productivity and other variables that can be affected by it. However, some of the things we never measure with time are tasks that are beneficial to us individually. We always measure how long we work as if it is our greatest achievement, but never how much time we get to spend with loved ones. Or we measure how much time we lose while waiting to be gratified, but rarely do we reflect on the kindness of others that saves us time, like when our partner does the dishes.

What we have created today is a lifestyle based on *tasks* that are often managed and measured by time. When we don't slow down to "stop and smell the roses" on a regular basis, we end up with a whole life full of time-flying-by moments. The mind can often wander off from what is happening presently and move onto what is coming next. The problem with this type of going too fast is that it can negatively influence us in the long term.

Humans today tend to measure success by the amount of time we put into something, not on the quality of what that something is. I often hear the words "I've put my time in." People want to measure the time they worked someplace or spent on a task. People use time to measure almost all things associated with actions such as work, exercising, and sports. What we don't see is people using time to organize individual tasks like hanging out with loved ones, recreation, education, or most other functions. The common habit of ignoring *personal* time makes us feel as if time has flown by. I believe that if we pay attention to the present moment, we will all slow down and begin to take control of time in our lives.

"Live in the present; the most important moment in your life is the present moment. It is in the present that all things are learned, lost, and forgotten." I wrote this back in the summer of 2017 when this book was just a twinkle in my mind. To this day, I often forget to stay focused on the present. Despite all my efforts to maintain the intention of staying present, I find myself digressing to thoughts of the future and the past on a regular basis. Perhaps this happens to you as well. Training yourself to live in the present moment is not an easy feat, but by acknowledging that you don't live in the present, you have already taken the first step toward *being* present.

Not living in the present moment and permitting our brains to be elsewhere—thinking—creates gaps in our memory where we have not fully absorbed what has happened in our surroundings. Training the mind to slow down and focus on our surroundings is not an easy task. You have to want it, to actively try to obtain it. You can begin by observing what is going on around you. What did you eat today? What conversations did you have? What emotions did you feel? What parts of life did you actively participate in and take notice of? To realize your potential individual influence—and the influence you have on others—you must slow down and experience life in the present with the knowledge of the past.

Learning to live in the present is a journey that lasts the rest of your life. Your ability to capture the present will come in fits and starts. Like any new habit, you will find yourself in uncharted territory and back to taking time (and yourself) for granted. Living in the present requires you to accept that this happens often and will probably happen for the rest of your life. However, the more you practice time management that works for you, the more you will see that living in the present slows life down; your memories and quality of life will be better.

If you gain control of the time in your life by living in the present, you can actually create a better life for yourself, and all those you influence. But you cannot regain time. Your past is the past. One second ago is now a part of who you are. Every second that goes by is another opportunity to achieve your dreams, to become who you want to be, to positively influence another person or yourself. You can do so much with your time—with your life. Do not waste it mindlessly, just going through the motions. Do not wake up in one, five, or even fifty years and wonder where your life has gone because your mind has been so lost in comfortable focus that you forgot to take the time to live. Living in the present moment is the art and act of slowing down. When *now* becomes a deliberate piece of your life, your life becomes clearer. Now is the time to gain control.

There are a number of ways to focus on the present moment. The first step is recognition of the time in your life you remember the least. For me, I often sit down with a pen and paper (or on my computer) and just write out my last few days—like a list.

A typical Monday to Friday for me at home looks like this:

6:00 a.m. Wake Up
6:10 a.m. Write in Journal
6:30 a.m. Exercise
6:45 a.m. Read Trade Rag Articles or Play a Mind Game
7:30 a.m. Make René Tea or Coffee
9:00 a.m. Leave for work
Office Time: This is where I lose track.

In fact, most days I cannot tell you what I have done after I arrive at work. This issue has persisted for as long as I can remember. I know that I proactively slow myself down at work numerous times throughout the day, but unless I review my working timeline where

I log my hours for clients, I cannot tell you what I do. What can really hurt anyone at this phase of life, and what we will discuss in the next section, is what many people think is an asset: multitasking.

Key Takeaways: Time Flies by So Quickly

- Time only moves at one speed in one direction; the only thing that changes is your perception. We all have the same amount of time.

- Measure your time in all areas, not just work. Be grateful for the time you get with friends or family, or for the time you can spend on recreational activities.

- To be in the now, know what to expect out of your day. Be prepared and plan your day at the start to give yourself the rest of your day to remain present.

The Turbo Charge of Going Too Fast

My advice on multitasking is this: don't do it. Ever.

One negative effect of losing your focus can be compounded by multitasking, which is also just another form of going too fast. We multitask to get more done in the same amount of time. Multitaskers are often celebrated for their ability to do so many tasks at once, but at what cost? The American Psychological Association states, "Doing more than one task at a time, especially more than one complex task, takes a toll on productivity."[2] We use contrasting parts of our brains to complete different tasks. When one part of our brain is focused on one specific task, the other parts of our brain are, essentially, muted. When we switch between tasks, this forces our brain to "jump-start" other areas of the brain for use. Switching tasks reduces productivity and increases the amount of time needed

---

2. (2006) "Multitasking: Switching costs" American Psychological Association. http://www.apa.org/research/action/multitask.aspx. Accessed 22 Feb 2018

to complete a task because it takes our brain time to switch gears and access the knowledge stored in different areas. Similarly, we cannot use our brain's power to give an equal amount of intense focus to several different tasks all at once. Focusing on multiple things at the same time diminishes our ability to access all of our stored knowledge for each specific task, in turn, reducing productivity and diminishing the quality of the final product.

Multitasking is synonymous with lying or stealing when it comes to work. *Stay with me here.* You're not really giving your full effort to that one task. Think about this: If you are paying for someone's time, and that person's attention strays to anything else during that time, would you receive a discount? If a plumber comes to your home and the job takes two hours of his time, one and a half hours spent working and the other thirty minutes spent answering phone calls or talking to you about the weather, would you receive a discount? What about the workers who text all day long, spending 20 seconds here and 20 seconds there?

The Pew Research Center conducted a study in which 1,035 participants were surveyed over the course of 10 or more study breaks. The study found that 97 percent of smartphone owners used their phones to text during their designated study period.[3] While this study was not at all surprising, as many people use their phones at work, at school, and mostly at home, it does show that people naturally take time to answer texts/DMs/emails on their phones while they are clocked in for work.

A good way to combat the turbocharge of going too fast is to plan out your day in advance. Set aside a few minutes in the morning (or the night before) to look over the tasks you have at hand for the day. Think about these questions while doing so: How many tasks do you *need* to finish by the end of your day? How long will each of your

3. (2015) "U.S. Smartphone Use in 2015" Pew Research Center. https://www.pewresearch.org/internet/2015/04/01/us-smartphone-use-in-2015. Accessed 22 Feb 2018

tasks take to complete? What is the priority and importance of each task? Which tasks will require the most brainpower? By answering these few questions, you will be able to plan out your day accordingly and steer clear of multitasking (making you more productive!).

Prioritize the tasks of higher importance for when you are most productive. You should tackle the tasks that require the most brainpower or have a close due date first. Next, work on the tasks that have a medium amount of importance but require a good amount of brainpower. You will want to schedule all your hardest and most challenging tasks when you are at your most focused, and save easy, brainless tasks (like replying to emails) for when you are least productive. Some individuals are most productive in the morning, while others are more productive at night. Get to know your rhythm and plan accordingly. Prioritizing will help keep you on task and will aid in productivity.

If it works for you, you can also try breaking up your day into segments once you have your task list for the day complete. Some people like to break their days up into thirty-minute increments, with one- to two-minute breaks in between to reset their brains. Others like to plow through a task and then take a short 10-minute break to give their brain a moment to switch gears to their next designated task. The important thing to remember is to give yourself regular and short brain breaks to ward off exhaustion.

Find what works for you. During your brain breaks, I recommend moving around a little bit. Even if it's just a quick walk around the office to fill up your water bottle, keeping the blood moving in your body will help your brain tremendously. While these short breaks may seem counterproductive, you will make up for this time with the added productivity you have by focusing on one task and avoiding multitasking.

It is imperative to note that every situation has an exception. The situations we discuss here are common, but there is always an exception to the rule. When you work in a position that doesn't allow you to focus on one specific task at a time, you need to have the capacity to work efficiently in that setting. You need to know that your specific job does not allow you to monotask. For example, as a receptionist, you may be interrupted frequently and quickly switch between tasks as the phone rings or as people come in to speak with you. This is inevitable in this kind of position, but the people who work productively in these positions are unique in their ability to resume the task they were working on prior to the interruption. They are able to plan for these disruptions and schedule their work accordingly.

It is also important to note that distractions *will* happen. When you are focusing on just one task, you may be disrupted. By not multitasking, you can focus on the task in front of you, and to understand that you may become distracted by things that are not in your control.

Key Takeaways: The Turbocharge of Going Too Fast

- Do your best not to multitask; it decreases productivity.

- Plan out your day in advance, either in the morning or the night before. (You may even choose to plan out your week rather than each day separately.)

  ○ How many tasks do you *need* to finish by the end of your day/week?

  ○ How long will each of your tasks take to complete?

  ○ What is the priority and importance of each of your tasks?

  ○ Which tasks will require the most brain power?

- Try breaking your day into segments (thirty minutes, an hour, by task, or whatever you prefer) and give your brain a rest between each.

- Be sure to schedule breaks throughout your day. Stretch, get some water, go for a walk, or do whatever helps you feel rejuvenated before starting again. We recommend getting your blood moving.

The Workplace

There is a gentleman who works in my office who, I swear, is always going a thousand miles per hour. When he walks through the office, he looks like he is training to race-walk in the 2022 Olympics. His hair is usually disheveled, and when you talk to him, he speaks hundreds of words per minute. Those of us who are in tune with him know that there is one way to slow him down—speak with him about fishing.

The transformation in him when we bring up fishing is amazing. His speech slows down, his body language changes, and he seems to regain some clarity. The conversation will seemingly go into slow motion because now we must endure his recap of some fishing story, and getting him out of this happy place can be difficult. Nonetheless, he will slow down and remain at that pace for the next hour or so—until his tunnel vision returns, and you see him fly by again, off to the races.

Our habit of speeding through life can negatively influence us at work. Going too fast can become cyclical, causing us and those we influence to speed up our lives in all aspects. Work speed can have a dramatic effect on us and those we influence in primarily negative ways.

Speed at work serves to reduce overall quality, as sloppy work is poor work. Speed in the workplace is only a requirement in professions like first response teams or medical personnel reacting to an accident or other medical emergency. However, for those of us in sales, management, and services, going fast does not lend itself to quality in any fashion.

I often get pushback from clients at this point: "What? You want me to slow down my staff?" Yes. I will ask, "What is so important that if staff took 15 percent longer to do that task, the company would be negatively affected?" I want to be clear here: Speed and focus are not synonymous. When we previously gave you the tools to focus more efficiently on each task at hand, that did not mean to speed through each task. It means to focus on each task. Speed sacrifices quality.

Of course, there are work environments that demand speed and it is accepted that quality suffers. Let's take a look.

Fast food service is an industry where speed is essential, and we accept a reduction in quality of product and service. The price of these products is such that procedure is the foundation of quality; if people follow procedure, then quality will follow. However, the demands of speed often override the advantages of procedure, and quality often suffers. How many times have you been to a fast-food restaurant and found too much of one ingredient in your food? The cause of this is speed. How many times have you opened the bag to see your food discombobulated in the packaging? The reason is how quickly the food was prepared. The demands to get the food out are flashing above the employee on a screen, screaming, "Go faster or the customer will be unhappy!" but the speed of action will itself make the customer unhappy.

Professional services are another industry that often demands speed. Legal, accounting, engineering, and management firms measure utilization as one of the key performance indicators (KPI). However, demands on timelines for clients often push us beyond what we are capable of. Then, we begin to rely on multitasking and co-mingling our mind power with action—often doing two, three, or four projects simultaneously. Multitasking results in missed tasks, inaccurate work product, and scope creep (digression from the main objectives) due to the re-work or additional resources needed to meet our obligations.

Sales involve processes. Some people are lucky enough to be in a field where the sales process is simple; the customer may come to the salesperson, and all that is needed is help setting up the delivery process for what is being purchased. Other sales require a lot more detail and often persuasion; this process can take hours, days, weeks, even months. However, in all sales, there is an urgency on the part of the salesperson, and perhaps on the customer as well. In the reactive sales process, the customer may rush through the process of buying an item or service, and due to this speed of action, they may not get what they really wanted. In that same situation, the salesperson, knowing that the sale will be quick and realizing that the customer is pressed to make a purchase, will often not ask questions that would clarify add-ons, changes, or other opportunities. The goal is to simply move past this sale and onto the next. In the long sales cycle, frustration in the process can lead to shortcuts, inadvertent misrepresentation—often caused by the speed of the sale—and lack of communication and understanding. Regardless of the result, the common denominator is speed of action.

Speed of action can actually result in avoidable delays; if we had just slowed down in the first place, we would have actually taken less time. A good example of this is if the customer or salesperson rushes through the ordering process and makes an error that results in sending the wrong item. The result is that it takes longer for the correct product to reach its destination, and the tasks will have been done twice because of going too fast the first time.

Another example is my son, Henry, who waits until the very last minute to get ready. Inevitably, in his rush, he forgets something that forces him to return home and take up twice as much time than if he had just slowed down. I myself do this at work if I'm rushing to a meeting; I forget things like my phone, cards, and notebooks.

I could provide examples for every single profession I have consulted with, but that would result in the writing of its own book. I am personally guilty of many of these examples and often excuse my behavior and the results. Regardless of who has caused the delay, I have to own the delay and the effect it has on my life and those I influence. I can either tackle the issue head-on and risk me speeding up or utilize my team to overcome the urge to speed up. Together, we are able to refocus our time, expectations, and performance in support of our goals of being deliberate. A proactive instead of a reactive approach allows us to have firm control of our immediate future.

Key Takeaways: The Workplace

- Speed at work serves to reduce overall quality, as sloppy work is poor work.
- Speed can result in delays if errors are made.
- Avoid procrastination to avoid the feeling of needing to speed through tasks.

S.M.A.R.T.

One of the best management tools for speed of action that I like to share with my clients is the S.M.A.R.T. (Specific, Measurable, Attainable, Realistic, Timely) process. For me and those I influence, S.M.A.R.T. is more than a goal; it is a verb that can be applied to all we do.

Specific

A lack of specificity while communicating can produce outcomes that are not intended. The people we correspond with do not have the privilege of reading our minds. The context we draw on to communicate is only known to ourselves, so we must do so with precision, until our point is 100 percent understood by the other party. Specificity requires you to slow down in order to achieve what you want in an accurate manner the first time.

Non-specificity creates confusion and can be very costly. It can lead to digression from the task (which is a time loss), inefficiency, and conflict. The consequences of non-specificity can range from fixable to catastrophic. I have known people to omit all negatives (consequences) from scope documents. However, a full understanding of the consequences is vital for reaching the true goal. You remain on the same page with all parties through specificity. Being specific will reduce the likelihood of scope creep (digression from the main objectives).

We once were contracted to develop an order management system for a large metal-building manufacturer. The system appeared to be pretty simple—this was back in 1999, prior to the complexity and tools now available via technology. This system was to be tied into the company's ERP system, which would take over the data management process of managing the design, manufacturing, packaging, delivery, and finalization of payment. The company had dealers around the country and wanted them to use a uniform order entry system that supported their business processes.

We had been supporting this client for a long time, and I had designed their ERP system. I spent many weeks at the client's factories around the United States, working side-by-side with their teams during the ERP development. I decided it would be best to hire an outside contractor to provide the computer programming to create this order entry system. However, due to my intimate understanding of the client's business, I wrote the scope documents for the programmer in verbiage that was quite vague.

My frustration with the programmers began when they did not seem to grasp the concepts behind what we were doing. My response to their persistent questioning was to tell them to go to the company's offices and ask for clarification. So, they went to the office, specifically to one of the new salespeople, and asked them what they would like to see in the program. These conversations led to other conversations with individuals who knew nothing about what we were trying to accomplish.

By not being specific about the scope, I had created an opening for errors. By not being specific about whom to talk to, I created an opening for scope creep. We ended up losing about six weeks of work because I was ambiguous. In not being specific and not paying attention, I allowed for this project to digress. We eventually learned from our error and got the project back on track.

Being specific does not end with the task description; it includes all aspects. Review clarity of message with anyone you delegate a task to or to whom you pass on critical information. By not being specific, context or details will get lost in communication. It's good practice to end these types of discussions with, "Do you understand _____?" and having them repeat back to you what it is they understand. If you are an individual who has been given a task and you do not understand, ask for clarification.

Finally, try to remember that people cannot read your mind. What's in your head and what you are trying to convey in conversation is clear to you, but those receiving the information may lack the context you have. Being specific is about providing that context for people so they understand what you are trying to communicate. You can achieve this by slowing down, using simpler words, getting to the point, asking them to repeat back to you how they understand your communication, and not digressing during conversations that convey important information.

Measurable

If you cannot measure it, you cannot control it. The act of measuring is another deliberate act of focus that supports slowing down. To measure, you need to be specific and create a way by which you can measure progress. KPIs are measurements that will force you to identify progress; writing down and reviewing your KPIs is an excellent proactive action if done regularly. When you set up a way to measure, you will slow yourself and the process down, ensuring that you are being proactive about identifying where you are in relation to your goal.

It's also very important to know what needs to be measured. Almost everything we do personally or professionally can be measured, but we often measure incorrectly. How do you choose a proper KPI? Well, that depends on your goal, which is unique to you, based on your position toward achieving that goal.

I'm going to use a personal issue that many are measuring today: steps. If the ultimate goal is to lose weight, measuring steps is only one KPI to focus on. If we reach our 10,000-step daily goal but still eat 3,500 calories and don't measure that, we may defeat our step goal. Our KPIs should include measuring calories and steps in order to achieve the ultimate goal of losing weight. Other KPIs that can be measured to achieve this goal are fat, protein, carb, or sugar intake.

Since we know what our goal is and what our limitations are, we can better plan our lives and schedules around these KPIs. Measuring for yourself will be difficult. We cheat ourselves and are our own worst support system when tasked with holding ourselves accountable; we can form all manner of excuses and justification for doing so. When developing measurement, ensure that you include some form of accountability.

Attainable

Your goals must be attainable with the resources you have. If you don't have the resources to meet your goal, you will take shortcuts (speed) that result in a product or service that does not measure up to your goal (unless your goal is to accept substandard results). Many people and organizations set unattainable goals. They do not take the time to understand what is needed and end up speeding through the process of goal setting, which ultimately creates unattainable goals. You must ensure that what you desire is attainable. If you are specific in what you want and can measure your progress, you likely have an attainable goal.

Some of the aspects of goal setting that are often unattainable are time, funding, support, and ROI (Return on Investment). For example, we often hear our clients ask for projects to be completed in a timeframe that is not conducive to producing optimal results. On the surface, these requests suffer from a lack of specificity. For example, a client may say, "I'd like to develop product X and have it to market in six months." Product X may be something they have already prepared for submission to vendors that can produce it, but at what cost? The client may have a limited budget, further making attainment more difficult. Or they may choose a price point that requires manufacturing to be outsourced to another country.

Each demand on its own may seem attainable. Can we make product X in six months? Yes. Can we bring product X to market on budget? Yes. Can we sell product X at the price point the market is dictating? Yes. Can we do them all at the same time? No.

When you have separate demands that are attainable on their own but not together, you will have to adjust some of the demands until they are all attainable. Being specific comes into play at this point. Within the details of specificity, we keep our tasks attainable.

Realistic

If you're not realistic, your goals will not be attainable. We need to ask ourselves, "Can I reach this goal with what I have available to me?" Have you been specific with what you need? Can you measure progress and keep track of the effort and assets required? Have you determined that what you want is attainable with your resources? Being realistic is difficult. Often, the reality of a situation is that we cannot do what we want.

There is a common issue in business that is caused by being unrealistic. I can honestly say that I address this issue with as many as 20 business owners a year and speak about these unrealistic expectations in one form or another during most of my presentations. I call this issue "bandwidth."

Most of us think of bandwidth as the capacity of data through a network; however, I use the term loosely to describe the capacity of just about anything. Business owners often think about one thing: sales. They push for sales above all other aspects of the business, and then bandwidth gets in the way. Sales are important but if owners and managers focus on sales without also focusing on the company's ability to fulfill those sales (bandwidth), there will be issues. When owners do this, they create other issues that further affect their ability to reach maximum efficiency. If owners align their sales bandwidth with their operational bandwidth (which is supported by the organization's administrative bandwidth), there will be operational integrity, which will maximize profits and success.

Let me provide a real-life example of what can happen when an organization is not prepared to support its sales growth. We once had a client who was an amazing carpenter. He worked strictly in office buildings and one day decided that he would start his own construction company. He leveraged his relationship with building managers into work. Then, he needed to hire some people to support him: laborers, a project coordinator, and office administration to start. He began with $200,000 in capital and was a natural salesperson. He quickly filled out his schedule but saw right away that he would run out of money, so he hired a project manager to sell more jobs and help him manage his current work.

Growth means more money, right? Wrong.

His company grew but he owed hundreds of thousands of dollars and had no available cash. He could not pay his employees or vendors. The stress caused him to project his frustrations on everyone he influenced. His drive to grow sales put him in a position that could cause bankruptcy, though he was flush with sales. Growing your business beyond your ability will result in a failure in your ability to perform the service, to collect for that service, and to address any issues that come up during that service. Any of these issues can kill a company.

Another area where being unrealistic is pervasive is the expectation to resolve problems. Most people face problem resolution in a totally reactive manner, so they only address the most visible aspect of the issue. Most individuals don't dive deeper to find the root cause. Without determining the root cause and rectifying the true issue, you create an unrealistic perception that the problem is solved.

As leaders, we often pressure our team to solve the most immediate issue and move on, not really giving support to the team to dig deeper. The expectation that we can lead in this manner and be effective is unrealistic. Eventually, the root cause issue will result in a bigger failure.

One of the most common effects of this is a loss of team members. Not empowering people with the time and resources to deal with the root cause of issues wears people out. Without looking to find the root of an issue, and following up by setting a measurable and attainable goal to resolve it, the team faces unrealistic expectations and demands.

For example, say we have an employee who is constantly missing deadlines. If we only address the issue of missing deadlines, our solution may be to take away some of that employee's tasks and reassign them to someone else, who then begins to miss deadlines. The reaction to this may once again be to move tasks to another person, re-creating the same issues. This may go on for a while, depending on the size of the company or the issues. Without actually looking at why the deadlines cannot be met, we never uncover the true issue.

We see this often in companies with distributed tasks, meaning that the company may rely on people to do multiple tasks, none of which are in support of the other required tasks. These people multitask through issues that are not connected, and the distraction of one is not in support of another. Further, the end results don't necessarily support any of the other tasks, leaving the person with a lack of support or connectivity. These people can be easily distracted and digress often from one task to another, never quite sure what is due when.

We can resolve these issues through business process reengineering or adding some simple task management tools. Other times, there needs to be a wholesale change in how the organization sets expectations for its employees or tasks. Setting realistic goals for employees means being specific, making them measurable, assuring they are attainable, and guaranteeing they are timely.

Timely

As I have discussed in a previous section, time is one thing that we can never seem to control. For one, time never stops for anything or anyone. If there is one pressing issue at work, it's time. Is the market ready for your product or service? Have you established a realistic timeline to reach your goals? Have you been specific about the time it takes to perform tasks, get information, or complete the actions needed? Can you measure the time needed? Is the timeline attainable, or do you have the resources needed to be timely in your efforts?

One of the companies that IA manages has eight patents. These patents are specific to the EPA (Environmental Protection Agency), NFPA (National Fire Protection Association), ANSI (American National Standards Institute), and IKECA (International Kitchen Exhaust Cleaning Association) standards, rules, and laws. It would be easy to assume that the products developed to resolve and meet these different organizational standards would provide a timely solution, but that would be wrong.

Next time you drive down a street full of restaurants, I want you to look at the fans on the rooftops (most look like mushrooms). You may see a dark streak leading from the fan. That is grease. The discharge of this grease is an issue for property and personal safety, groundwater contamination, and it is also a fire hazard. Look at the used grease dumpsters in the back of those same restaurants; you will notice a similar streak leading away—more of the same issues as on the roof. Patents and products to address these issues have been available to solution providers for the past 30 years, yet 85 percent of all restaurants are not in compliance.

Why is this issue not providing timely access to the manufacturers and service providers who resolve them? Accountability. While these rules and regulations are in place, most of the market is not being held accountable. The providers often create ad hoc solutions not designed to properly contain or support the grease containment.

A manufacturer who sees the problem and reads the rules may feel they are being timely; not in this case. Because the AHJ (Authorities Having Jurisdiction), such as the fire marshals, building code inspectors, and groundwater managers, are not really looking at the root cause, the market is not demanding proper resolutions from the service providers. Thus, we have 85 percent noncompliance and no accountability. Innovation in this space is lacking.

Making S.M.A.R.T. a Verb

The lack of accountability is duplicated across countless issues facing us today. However, one of the answers to a lack of accountability is applying S.M.A.R.T. to our daily lives, tackling the root cause as an Individual team, and using our influence positively. When we specifically conduct our decisions, communication, and actions in a measured, attainable, realistic, and timely manner, we solidify our ability to be a positive influence. S.M.A.R.T. can and should be applied to everything in your daily life. In doing so, you can affirm that you are doing your best and attempting to examine all variables at play.

Key Takeaways: S.M.A.R.T.

- If you engage in S.M.A.R.T., all areas of your life will benefit.
- Specific:
  - A lack of specificity can produce unintended outcomes.
  - Being specific will reduce the likelihood of scope creep (digression from the main objectives).
  - When communicating specificities, slow down, use simple words, get to the point, don't digress, and ask the other party to repeat the details back to you in their own words.

- Measurable:
  - If you cannot measure it, you cannot control it.
  - Choose proper key performance indicators (KPIs) that depend on your goal and are based on where you are now compared to where you want to be.
- Attainable:
  - Your goal must be attainable with the resources you have.
  - If you are specific and can easily measure progress, your goal is likely attainable.
  - Some aspects of goal setting that are often unattainable are time, funding, support, and return on investment (ROI).
  - When you have separate tasks that are part of your goal and are attainable on their own but not together, you will have to adjust some of the demands until they are all attainable.
- Realistic:
  - If you're not realistic, your goals will not be attainable.
  - If any problems occur, get to the root of the problem to ensure your goal stays realistic. Not knowing the root of a problem could lead to skewed perceptions, ultimately making your goal unrealistic without your knowledge.
- Timely:
  - Establish a realistic timeline to reach your goals.
  - Be specific about the time it takes to perform tasks, get information, and complete necessary actions.
  - Ensure the timeline is attainable and acquire the resources needed to be timely.

Reaction

Speed also often interferes with our reactions to stimuli in our environment, whether from ourselves, others, or random happenings in our vicinity. There are times when our reactions are good, but there are also times when our reactions can harm ourselves and others. Often, these negative reactions occur due to negative *emotions*. These emotions can interfere with our ability to be a positive influence, which may disrupt our flow of opportunity. Reactive and emotional tendencies can alienate us from people or situations that might otherwise provide advantages to us. How many times have you overreacted to an issue and, in doing so, changed your life path?

Back in the mid-1990s, I sold my first company, Business Accounting Solutions. When I sold this company, I worked for a few additional companies as a contractor. During that time, I traveled a lot between San Francisco and Denver, and the expenses were quite high. As a contractor for companies, I billed for my time and expenses. One day, I received a check for about half of what they owed me, which was unexpected. When I called, I was informed that there was a chance that I would not be paid any more funds. My reaction was purely emotional.

Having a direct relationship with the CEO of the company, I went down to their offices to meet with him and immediately took an emotional posture. I informed him how it *should* be and, in so many words, how it *would* be if he did not pay me the full amount. He informed me that the company had money issues, that the check in my hand was all he could promise, and that it very likely represented the full amount they would ever pay me. He also told me that they did not disagree with what was fully owed, but that this was a matter of his company's survival.

My reaction to his calm demeanor was to get angrier. I reacted to his ability to look me in the eye and tell me he was not going to pay me. During the time he was explaining his company's position, all I thought about was the money he was withholding from me. My mind was calculating the loss, and the loss was feeding my anger, and my anger was feeding my mouth with words that were unprofessional and, quite frankly, only hurting me.

My last action of the day with this client was to reach across his desk, grab a pen, and write VOID on the check he had given me. I threw his check at him and told him that he owed me the full amount and that I would collect my money one way or another. My client looked at me almost comedically, but I suspect from what I know today, it was pity. While he looked at me, he calmly said, "Do what you feel is right for your company, but I think our business here is finished."

I was so angry that I stormed out of the office, and my first call was to my attorney. During my call to the attorney, my emotions began to subside, and I reviewed the events that had transpired. My attorney calmly interrupted, "Did you keep the check they gave you?" My answer was only about halfway out of my mouth when it hit me: I had thrown away over $3,500.

That company closed shortly thereafter. Some other company got my money, and I got an expensive lesson in managing my emotions. Later in this book, you will learn how the next reactive moment in my life would cost me millions of dollars *and* a friendship.

There is a moment after we have made a mistake, after the consequence has set in, where we look back and ask, "How did this happen?", only to realize that the information we could have used to avoid this issue was there all along. We were only going too fast to realize it then. What opportunities have you now missed because of this mistake?

Key Takeaways: Reaction

- Negative emotions can interfere with our ability to create advantages or opportunities if we have reactive tendencies.

Identify reactive tendencies that disrupt you or others you influence.

- If you feel the need to react immediately, take a pause. How you create a moment to pause and what you do with that moment will bring you back to the present moment and allow you to think about your response more clearly.

- If you still struggle with reactive tendencies, solicit someone to hold you accountable to those tendencies and engage you in understanding the root cause.

Focus Reflection

The act of slowing down and focusing on the present moment can be one of the most amazing moments in your life. That first act of pause can give you an epiphany, the clarity of thought for your "ah-ha" moment to focus on the issue at hand. A pause can bring focus to a past issue, which can be used as a tool going forward and living in your present moment. To realize your own individual advantages, and to learn all you can from your life experience and that of others, you must focus on your present moment. Take the time to find what it is that helps you slow down enough to become present, whatever that might be. Talk about fishing, take a hot shower, play a video game, meditate, work out, cook, write, draw, or whatever gives you pause—slow down to realize your full potential.

CHAPTER 4

WHO AM I?

"Our vision will
become clear only
when you can look
into your own heart.
Who looks outside,
dreams; who looks
inside, awakes."
—Carl Jung

Have you ever looked into a mirror
and thought, "Who am I?"

One of the consequences of going
too fast in our lives is that we lose track
of who we are. When we begin to slow
down, not only does our present life
come into focus but our past life does
as well. I can honestly say that up to
the age of about 30, I did not reflect on
my childhood or where I came from. I
did not sit and contemplate the influence my past had on who I was, other
than maybe my education or work
experience.

That said, my childhood created
the foundation of who I am today. My
foundation includes flaws and opportunities that have changed the direction

of my life many times in my 56 years. My past is filled with joy, sorrow, regret, anticipation, love, and loss—emotions that add to my lived experiences of education and other learned lessons. Even as I sit here and write this book, I am struck by the question, "Who is Brian Smith?" Maybe a better question is, "Who do I want to be?" Some may wonder if it is appropriate to ask myself this question at this stage in my life. However, I think this is an appropriate question to ask at any stage of life. In fact, it should be one you continually ask yourself to ensure you are on the path you want to be on.

I'm going to digress from my original question above for a moment: "Who is Brian Smith?" Not too long ago, I was with a client whose team kept asking me, "Why do you want to help us?" (I get this question a lot.) This client is a large food manufacturing company that is almost a hundred years old and still in the same family. The company is amazing, built on the backs of employees who have dedicated their working lives to it. When I answered this question with, "It's what I like to do," that was not enough for many of their leaders. They wanted a more complex answer.

I like what I do because I get to help people realize who they are and give them an opportunity to either accept themselves or make changes. When I work with people, they always get something from me—either validation of their current situation or information that leads to some new direction, even if I am not involved in that new direction. Many companies move on without my team and me and find a way to alter what they have been doing. Other times, they just keep doing what they were doing. Sometimes this choice to continue on with the status quo results in stagnated growth, an increase in negative situations, or even going out of business.

The following example is indicative of what we often face as consultants. One day, one of our team members introduced me to a new potential client. This man sat in my office and outlined his business issues (which were quite daunting). During the discussion, the client boasted about his math skills and the incredibly complex spreadsheets he created to manage his business (which was failing).

After the entire story had been outlined to the satisfaction of my potential client and me, I told him we could help him, but it would cost about $35,000. I told him I would provide a detailed project plan to identify how we would help him and in what timeframe, and I asked for a $5,000 retainer.

The potential client made a choice not to use us. He also ignored some of the detrimental information that came to light during our two-hour meeting. Two months later, he was sitting in front of me with his primary shareholder, asking me to go over the plan I had mentioned two months prior. However, circumstances had changed for him and his company. Two months prior, he had been in debt but not in default; now, he was in default with his creditors and could not pay his employees. It was four days before Christmas.

This man had 37 employees, most of whom lived paycheck to paycheck. I knew that if I did not help him, all 37 people and their families would be dramatically affected. I reiterated what I told him the first time but informed him that the price would go up. The reason? Taking him on as a client now meant that we needed to get his staff paid and affect change quickly. If left to his own devices, he would fail.

We came to an agreement, and the next day I walked into the client's office and handed each employee a paycheck three days before Christmas. The client stood next to me and explained that we wanted them to focus on their families for the holidays but to return to work afterward with renewed spirit. Together we would ensure that this would never happen again in this company.

Eight months later, all thirty-seven employees were still employed there. We sold that company to a larger one, ensuring that the business plan and people working toward its success were stable. Today that company is surpassing its objectives and has increased its workforce.

This story exemplifies why I do what I do and why I try to find a way to influence people; I believe that I have an ability to assist people in realizing their potential, both individually and Individually (collectively).

Now, back to my previous question: "Who do I want to be?"

I *am* who I want to be! At work, I am the guy who helps (I)individuals find who they are and realize that they can be whoever they want to be within the context of their effort and abilities. To be the person that you want to be, at work or at home, you have to understand yourself on all levels. To understand yourself to this degree means that you understand, or at least recognize, that you have an inner *and* an outer you.

My experience has shown me that there are basically two of each of us: who we are on the inside and who we are on the surface. Now, I don't mean this to imply that people are purposefully fake; I mean this generally in a healthy way. People are not always what you see during your interactions with them. We are all made up of our experiences, both good and bad. Our past influences who we are, yet we cannot wear those experiences on our sleeves all the time.

For example, how many times have you experienced something that you knew was just ridiculous, but you couldn't state your true feelings out loud? It may be a rare occurrence, but we've all been there—we accidentally blurt out our opinion on what we have just witnessed. Unfortunately, this may not be positive or match what people know of us, and we immediately think to ourselves, *Oops. Did I just say that out loud?* Some days it's more difficult to have self-control, as you will read in my example below.

This occurrence is a glimpse of the inner self. Generally, this is the part of us we like to keep inside, or at least reserve for those who are, in our minds, safe to share that part with. Then there is the outer you. This is the person most people know you to be. Often, there is a great divide between what we portray in our day-to-day life and what is really inside. Some of this dissension can be found on the surface.

I used to fly to Illinois once a month from Oregon. I did this from September 2010 to June 2013, when we finally moved to

Illinois permanently. During my trips, I had the opportunity to meet with two men who graduated from the high school I attended in ninth grade. The circumstances of this meeting were that my client in Illinois had grown up with these men and, at one time, had been their partner. My client is a fairly grounded person; he is, to a certain extent, fiscally responsible. As I sat and listened to his former partners brag about their assets, I remembered some data I had recently seen about these two, specifically about the extent of their debt.

About halfway through lunch, one of the partners looked at my client and said, "Is that a Timex watch?" My client, looking down at this watch, just answered with a simple "yes." The former partner quickly produced his watch, a beautiful Swiss timepiece, and confided that he had just purchased it for $160,000. My reply was so immediate it even shocked me: "Maybe that's why you are millions of dollars in debt."

Now, I don't begrudge people spending their money on nice things. I am a capitalist and believe in the free market. However, pretentiousness in the face of self-deprecating actions and stupid assertions makes me crazy. By this I mean that there are people out there who risk security for themselves and their families to fulfill a need to be pretentious. Like in my example above, spending $160,000 on a watch is something done for self-fulfillment. On a less grand scale, people may buy cars, homes, or clothes in support of similar needs but to the detriment of their financial or emotional well-being.

Understanding oneself begins with one often forgotten fact: we all have an ego. Understanding that this is something wholly human is our first step to understanding the complexity of what ego does to the question "Who am I?"

Ego

What is ego? Ego is purely human. Ego drives our personality, communication, and perceptions. Ego can be complementary or damaging.

Ego is your sense of identity, and it can help *and* hinder you. Ego is your self-esteem or, for some, your self-worth. Perception can play a huge factor in what you or others perceive as your ego. Behind a camera, many become shy or come to life, while off-camera, they feel the opposite—lively or introverted. Different contexts reveal different facets of our ego.

Our ego is driven by many factors. It can be driven by our physical appearance, such as being good looking, fit, or put together. Ego can be driven by our education, income level, or social crowd. Ego can be influenced by us or by others. Ego is something that can be propped up in a flash and then taken away just as quickly. Ego can feel good to some, but the perception of that ego can make others feel bad.

We used to have an associate with an amazingly large ego. This associate is what some would typically call a "pretty human," with good looks, well-spoken, and generally above-average intelligence. If you worked with this person, you would be impressed by his organizational image; his look is clean and tidy. In fact, this person would describe himself as having the "Clark Kent" look.

However, wherever this person goes, there is a path of wonderment in his wake: How can someone with such talent and opportunity allow his inner self to emotionally and physically conflict with his outer self? On the outside, he gives the impression of being neat and tidy, yet, on the inside, he is highly disorganized and dirty.

I once got into his car, and it was absolutely filthy. Not cluttered, but filthy. When I brought this to his attention, his excuse was that it was an old car, and no one was ever in it. However, a week later, I saw him with his kids in that car. That image stayed with me. Intermingled with that impression were memories of this associate's poor interactions with others. Those interactions usually indicated that he had no issue with his massive outer ego.

Fast forward to when the associate bought his dream car. About a month after the car was purchased, we had an opportunity to ride together on the way to see a client, and I let him drive. This new luxury car was spotless on the outside, but as soon as I opened the door, it was pure filth—*again*. It was dusty, dirty, and messy and smelled of sweat, dirt, and fast food.

The contrast between the outside of the car and the inside was much like the contrast embodied by this person. On the outside was a superficial exterior that looked and sounded good; however, on the inside, there was chaos. On that same drive, he immediately put on what I believe would be classified as "gangster rap" and began to drive aggressively. Now, I don't care what kind of music anyone listens to. I myself have a very eclectic playlist that includes artists such as Eminem, Tool, Katy Perry, Disturbed, Foo Fighters, Lindsey Stirling, and Mozart. I am also no Sunday driver. I enjoy my cars and tend to lean on the more aggressive side of driving.

However, the volume of the music was turned up after we began driving. When driving with any team member on the way to see a client or otherwise, my approach is to be respectful and not immediately turn up my music. However, I wish it stopped there. We then took off like we were rushing to a fire.

I turned down the music on my own: "Really? Full volume?" The reaction I got to my words was a look of incredulousness, as if he were saying, *How dare you touch my car or tell me how loud my music should be?* This all occurred as we sped away from our office at 70 miles per hour in a 35 mile-per-hour zone.

I made a comment about his driving and received the same incredulous look. While our drive continued, I began to inquire as to why his brand-new dream car was so dirty and why he drove so poorly; his non-answer and look of confusion as to why I would even ask answered my question. The final kicker was our turn toward the client: a high school business incubator team. (Each year, the high school that my son attended has a team of kids who create their own potential companies. We help them with the logistics of the business, and at the end of the program, they pitch to a "shark team" and are awarded money for their ideas.) We were in a school zone, and as we blasted through at 60 miles per hour, I could not help but feel empathy for this person and his ego.

This story may have you wondering, *What could this possibly have to do with who I am?* Well, your inner self or subconscious can manifest itself in strange ways. For this person, his ego manifested itself in a dirty car and erratic driving. When confronted, he had an excuse for every action or lack of action; the dirty car was a result of a lack of time and the bad driving was a result of me being an old "fuddy-duddy." In reality, he only thought about himself.

What's inside influences what's outside. Many of us protect the outside from our inside; what we think is not what we say. If we allow ego to negatively influence us, then the risk of showing those parts of us that we don't want the general public to see goes way up.

If you really want to grow, then you need to face your own demons. You need to reconcile how others see you, how you *want* others to see you, and who you want to be when you are alone. During this reconciliation process, you may not like what you see; in fact, it may scare the living bejesus out of you. But if your goal is to be someone you are not today, then you must go through the entire process to be that person. If you find that living one way and being another is exhausting or creating chaos in your life, begin with being honest about the contradictions you live with.

To see yourself clearly in the mirror, you must become humble. One of the best ways to learn about yourself is to ask others. Stop, slow down, and take inventory of your most common places. Stop and look around at where you sleep, where you shower, where you eat, and where you drive. Stop and look around your workplace. Ask your peers, especially those who rely on you for something, "What traits do you see in me that I might want to work on?"

Have you ever been called selfish? If you have, you may want to ask yourself why. Instead of a quick reactive justification, seek to ask what could label you as selfish. Have you ever been called arrogant? Again, why would someone call you this? Do you justify your arrogance under the guise that you're just that good? Does being "that good" mean that you should exhibit arrogance as a by-product of being good?

Do you react in anger to things that don't go your own way? Why? Is your ego so large that you feel that anger is the only way to communicate your displeasure? Does anger deliver your message better than empathy? I used to wear the badge of being labeled an asshole like it was some medal of honor. My justification (ego) said that I could do this as long as I was honest about my "asshole" actions. Really? There is no human on Earth who has earned the right to treat another human being poorly; that is just not something we should be proud of.

Another ego-driven trait is impatience. I have been guilty of this. Knowing what I know, and at times expecting others to know what I know, does not give me the right to flex my ego in the form of impatience. Impatience is one of the ego-driven issues that can cause us to make others speed up, and we have already clearly outlined what speeding up can do to us.

Ego drives more bad decisions than it does good ones. However, ego is not all bad. Ego also provides us with a means to keep moving forward. One of the best examples of ego gone right *and* wrong is sports.

In professional baseball, the best hitters can fail more than two-thirds of their times at-bat. Good hitters have batting averages in the range of .300 to .350. As children, these hitters may have exhibited batting averages closer to .400 or even .500. Overperformance like this builds the ego. It is this same ego that carries this individual into a professional career where failure two-thirds of the time is acceptable.

This metric for failure is also seen in basketball, football, hockey, and soccer; failure outpaces success at the micro-level of play throughout. Yet the one thing that keeps these professionals going, besides the million-dollar paychecks, is their ego. Sadly, that same ego creates arrogant sports figures who feel entitled to use that fame and fortune to spread conflict, turmoil, and overall negative influence. We hear about cheating, abuse, and excess that is destructive to the players, their families, and their fans, who often emulate their behavior.

The final display of the negative and positive impact of the ego is in politics. I am of the opinion that 20 percent of all politicians are narcissists fed by their egos. These 20 percent ruin the political atmosphere. Think about this: Of all the members of current and past Congress and presidents, how many do we actually hear from on a regular basis? When you really think about these vocal and "active" politicians, a high percentage of them are so opinionated that they lack understanding of what is really happening at the grassroots level. They are enamored with their own voice and reflection and don't really connect with most Americans. Yet the media, in its own egotistical actions, prop up those that are the most egotistical as if they are the only ones who speak for us citizenry. Quietly, however, behind the scenes, the other 80 percent try to accomplish what they can for their constituents, those who live in the states or districts within the states that the members represent. Yet, these positive politicians are less discussed.

Ego is what drives this system. Listen to some politicians speak; they will say "I" far more than "we" or "us." Look at how they act and vote; their words are more about their beliefs, not the beliefs of the people they represent. Whenever I see state representatives pushing a message nationally, I always question their motivation; I ask, "What does this have to do with where they are from? Who gains from their actions: the politician and his party, or the people they represent?" Then I ask, "How do I choose what is important to me, and what is driving my decisions to be vocal?" At this moment, I look in the mirror and challenge myself to be true, not only to me but to those I influence directly as well. I encourage you to do the same.

Key Takeaways: Ego

- Ego is your sense of identity, and it can be complementary or damaging to your influence.

- We all have an ego. It is an important part of who you are and is a key part of being human.

- Know your ego and realize its importance as well as its risks.

- Be respectful of those who are experiencing life around you. Consider how your actions may influence them.

- What's inside influences the outside. If you want to grow, face your demons and the things that hold you back.

- If you want to learn about yourself, ask others about their perceptions of you.

- Be mindful of impatience, as impatience is usually ego-driven.

Self-Reflection: Looking at Your Internal Mirror

The first time I attempted to reflect on my past, I can honestly say it scared me.[4] To this day, there is a huge black hole in my childhood. In 2014, I moved my family back to the area in Illinois where I grew up. Today, I am surrounded by the people I grew up with, some of them since I was five years old. Every day of the workweek, I drive through West Dundee and see the homes where I grew up. These interactions have helped to shine a light into that black hole and catch a glimpse of memories that continue to refine who I am today.

My advice for self-recollection is writing or documenting a life timeline. (I suggest documenting your life in a timeline-like form with events that occurred over the years. You will see an example of mine shortly.) My original recollection activity was centered around my insecurity about change.

In 1996, when I started IA, we lived in our first Thornton, Colorado home. At the time, that home was in a state of disrepair;

---

4. The act of self-reflection may recall things that are unpleasant and may require counsel from a professional psychologist. Self-reflection may uncover the root of personality traits that include abuses or incidents of trauma that trigger subsequent mental health issues. If you are or become aware of any memories that cause you any mental trauma or distress, please seek help immediately.

we were fixing it up, and my life at home and work was in a constant state of change. I was still working for someone else—these were the early days of IA, when we built its foundation.

My primary career at the time was Worldwide IT Manager for a global oil exploration company. The company was traded publicly on the NASDAQ, and my work was very visible; I was designing and implementing the computer and ERP systems worldwide. I was 30 years old in a world full of professionals. While I was very good at IT and ERP, I was *not* good at interacting with professionals from large, nine-figure, publicly traded companies.

The anxiety I felt seemed, at first, to be all mine. However, as I traveled the world implementing our systems in quiet corners like Mount Gilead, Ohio, Jamestown, North Dakota, and Los Reyes, Mexico, I began to experience that same anxiety from the people working at the companies we were acquiring. However, my peers, or people with similar education and ages, in places like Houston, Texas, Calgary, Alberta, and New York City had almost no anxiety.

Since my early IA work was focused on developing a standardized procedure to understand, document, and adapt business processes and manage change in organizations, I was acutely aware of the anxiety and worked to identify its root cause. From the first day I felt anxiety in myself, I began to self-reflect; this is when I developed my timeline review, or what has now evolved into BizVision.

Self-reflection begins with a timeline from birth to today. The first timeline review of my life was, in and of itself, revealing. I had never performed this act for myself because any time I thought about my childhood, all I got was a mind full of nothing. But, while sitting at a desk writing out my timeline in 1996, I got this:

1966: Born to young parents - Elgin, Illinois (Mom 16, Dad 20) (Sherman Hospital)
Kindergarten: Immanuel Lutheran - East Dundee, Illinois (Age?) (5) (5–6) (1971–1972) (Move)

1st Grade: Immanuel Lutheran - East Dundee, Illinois (Age 6–7) (1972–1973) (Stayed with my teacher at her home, felt secure)
2nd Grade: Immanuel Lutheran - East Dundee, Illinois (Age 7–8) (1973–1974)
3rd Grade: Immanuel Lutheran - East Dundee, Illinois (Age 8–9) (1974–1975)

By the way, each parenthetical term or phrase represents another recollection that had occurred. This happened in a single sitting, not over a long period of time.

4th Grade: Immanuel Lutheran - East Dundee, Illinois (Age 9–10) (1975–1976) (Kiss first girl) (Call teacher a bitch, get hit in head by her)

Here is where my first "ah-ha" moment occurred!

4th Grade: Move to Wood Dale, Illinois (Parents split up) (We live with aunt) (Zion Lutheran School) (Age 9, 1975) (Hit in head by teacher)
5th Grade: Move to Itasca, Illinois (Age 10–11) (1975–1976) (No baseball) (Live in apartments) (Ridiculed by kids at St. Luke Lutheran)
6th Grade: Move back to Dundee, Illinois (Parents get remarried) (Age 11–12) (1976–1977)
7th Grade: Immanuel Lutheran - East Dundee, Illinois (Parents get divorced) (Mom leaves for California) (Age 12–13) (Move)
7th Grade: Move to California in April (Attend first public school, Los Cerritos, in Thousand Oaks, California) (Age 13) (New stepfather)
8th Grade: Move back to Dundee, Illinois (Stay in public schools: Dundee Middle School) (New stepmother is 20, my age 13–14)
9th Grade: Dundee High School - Carpentersville, Illinois (New brother) (Strive for friends and am part of "in" group at DHS) (Age 14–15)

10th Grade: Move to Thousand Oaks, California (Attend Thousand Oaks High School) (Age 15–16)

11th Grade: Thousand Oaks High School - Thousand Oaks, California (Age 16–17)

12th Grade: Thousand Oaks High School - Thousand Oaks, California (Age 17–18)

That entire exercise took me about five minutes, but it opened up my mind to things I had not thought about. For example, my "ah-ha" moment was: *Wow, I moved a lot.*

Mapping yourself does not need to be a complex process. I've seen books and other advisors advocate mapping out your entire self and creating a large list to focus on. As you are aware, I am of the opinion that multitasking is a very bad thing. This means that influencing change in yourself needs to be singular in action; get one thing fixed and move on to the next.

To this day, I cannot recall how I felt back in grade school. But I have added to my timeline over the past 26 years, especially since moving back to where I spent many of my early years. What I initially realized back in 1996 was that my anxiety was fueled by eight moves from kindergarten to twelfth grade and seven schools, including three elementary, two middle, and two high schools. Also, my parents divorced, remarried each other, divorced again, remarried other people, and then added to our family. As you can probably imagine, my anxiety about change became clear in that first five-minute recollection.

Identifying the root of an issue is not always easy. Furthermore, what do we do with that knowledge once we have it? I know that, for me, as soon as I identified what was causing my anxiety about change at the core, that anxiety was not as intense the next time it was triggered. You may find the same happens for you; identifying the root of something or accurately categorizing our emotions can often make them more manageable, which can lead to them feeling less intense in future situations. At the very least, this knowledge allows us to be more aware and present.

As Worldwide IT Manager for a global oil exploration company at the age of 30, I continued to search for a way to incorporate my new knowledge and use it to develop a way to influence and manage change in the workplace. The most obvious way to me was to finish my timeline, add to it, and expand the influence of my past over who I was. I wanted to know: what made me such a natural salesperson? What drove me to work hard but procrastinate the most important tasks until almost the last moment? Why did I have a propensity to listen to others? How was it that at age 30, without any real mentor, I could be so pragmatic about business issues? And why did I hate surprises, any kind of surprises?

Self-reflection is also about understanding your everyday actions and reactions. The questions I initially came up with were for those things that were at the top of my mind at the time. As my life has changed, my questions have changed, and the challenge of self-reflection repeats itself.

As I write this book and look at my team's comments throughout my writing, I feel stuck in identifying how to guide such a personal and inward-looking task as self-reflection to the various people who will be reading this and applying it. I think the first question you should tackle is, *Why am I self-reflecting?*

What is challenging you to discover or rediscover yourself? As you determine the root cause of your desire to self-reflect, begin to write down those thoughts, feelings, and challenges in a journal or someplace where you can read it back to yourself. The act of finding what is driving you to self-reflect may prove simple or amazingly daunting; whatever it is, continue to let your mind flow and write down what your mind brings you.

When I did this, I was led to create a timeline. Time is something we all can follow, and a timeline can trigger memories, good and bad. Nonetheless, it's what began my journey. For you, it may not be a timeline but a single event. The events may be few and far between; regardless, once you begin to write them down, you have a puzzle on paper that you can fill in as you go. It may or may not be date sequential; in fact, I have often been focused on an event that happened in my 30s only to be bounced to a memory from my childhood. That is how the human mind works—randomly—and why I recommend writing it all down.

Other questions you can ask yourself:

- *Why am I friends with _____?*
- *Why do I live in _____?*
- *Why did I make the decision to _____?*
- *What influences me to be _____?*
- *Why am I influenced by the things that influence me?*

For context, I know why I live in Illinois. I know why I choose to remain friends with people whom others may deem unwise to associate with. I know why I make decisions; sometimes it's for selfish reasons and other times it's not, but I understand my decision-making process now. I know what influences me, good and bad.

Self-reflection will be one of the most intimate things you will ever do. It may scare you. It may anger you. But it will change you. Only you can control what you ask yourself. You can choose not to write things down and risk maintaining those gaps in your life that, if answered, may help you or those you influence. In the end, self-reflection is about accepting who you are at the moment you ask those questions because regardless of who you are now, you *will* be different tomorrow.

Key Takeaways: Self-Reflection: Looking at Your Internal Mirror

- Ask yourself: Why am I choosing to reflect on myself now? What do I want to accomplish from personal reflection?

- Create a life timeline to begin your self-recollection process. Looking back at your life in a chronological manner can help maintain perspective, provide context, and discover hidden influences.

- When working on yourself, choose one thing to focus on at a time.

- If you feel inclined, write down your journey in a journal.

Roots

Earlier I mentioned that a client recently asked me why I do what I do, or why I want to help them. The question came about during a discussion about organizational development and realizing their value proposition to their organization. The client asked me why I would spend a full day working with their type of company, then fly to Dallas the next day to work with another small company, then turn around and fly back to them the next day. Essentially, the client wanted to know why I would do all of this when I am the owner of a consulting firm and many other companies.

My answer was simple: I like consulting. However, the three people asking me were executives at a large manufacturing company. They were looking for what motivated me on a deeper level. During my self-reflection, I learned that I was often left alone to make decisions and fend for myself. I had to find a way to overcome the generalizations and stereotypes that went along with my particular situation. Working only for the money is as shallow as dating a good-looking person only because they have good looks. I realized a long time ago that I did not want others to feel the isolation that comes when you're left to solve problems you're not quite capable of solving on your own.

It is this motivation that has created my passion for helping people be the best they can be for the companies they work with. There are many ways to help people, but at work, people face challenges unique to human development. We all need work to meet the most basic needs of our lives: food, shelter, and security. If we are unsuccessful in our ability to be effective at work, we risk our very livelihoods. I have learned that providing people with the best opportunity to be self-sufficient and helping them be the most productive they can be at work will help to ensure that their basic human needs stay fulfilled.

As my motivation carried me from company to company, my understanding of the complexity of human interaction and the challenges businesses face in creating environments for us to work together effectively was transparent. My passion to help others understand how to do and be better for themselves and their company is deeply rooted in my childhood.

This passion has led me to a lot of dead ends, and I often felt like I was in a maze, not really knowing where I was going or how to get there. The challenges of developing myself often interfered with my motivation and replaced my passion with single-mindedness and loathing. Upon reflection, I realized that this depletion was because I was experiencing the same types of rejection from the people I was trying to benefit as I received as a child from the kids who would not accept me. When I was a child, I had to find ways to manipulate the situation to be accepted. I figured, surely, I could do the same thing as an adult.

In my younger days, I bragged and pretended to be someone I was not as a way to overcome the rejection of my peers. I felt that if I could fit in without actually having the socio-economic foundation to do so, I could overcome the challenges I was facing.

When René and I were younger, we became friends with a couple who were a little older than us and had a child a few years older than Mary. This couple had affluent parents, and it showed—from the cars they drove to the clothes they wore to the friends they kept. This couple introduced us to their friends; all of them were, generally speaking, snobs.

Still, René and I looked up to these people and did all we could to fit in. However, we did not have the resources to keep up with the pace of this group. We ended up making rash decisions, and we overspent on things to appear to be more like them. When we were together, I would talk about the wins I had, even exaggerating those wins to elevate my stories to a level these people could accept and respect. Nonetheless, they saw right through it and never quite accepted us.

Throughout my life, my cycles of trying to fit in have ultimately taught me how to accept who I am, and it has shown me what my value proposition is to my family, friends, companies, and clients. Value is not a dollar amount; it's the reward we get from achieving our goals, the thing that motivates us to keep doing what we like and find a way to shed that which we don't like.

Self-realization is about linking your motivation to your experiences and finding the passion within to propel you forward—one moment at a time. Self-realization is your chance to reframe the events that you feel have been holding you back and turn them into the fuel that drives you to the next phase of learning and growth. Self-realization is using those memories to stay the course and not digress or abandon that which you know is right and good. Self-realization is identifying your mistakes and not repeating them but working out solutions for them. By equipping yourself with the truth of your foundation through self-realization, it is easier to know who you want to be.

Key Takeaways: Roots

- Consider where you came from and how your upbringing has influenced who you are today, in ways that may or may not be obvious.

- Self-realization is about linking your motivation to your experiences and finding the passion to propel you forward, one moment at a time.

Who Do You Want to Be?

I think it's humorous when people ask children who or what they want to be when they grow up. The innocence of the answers from children reminds us that life should be so simple as to choose our future purely on the basis of the passion we feel. Children answer these questions knowing only that being a policeman, fireman, or what their parents do makes them feel, generally, very good. Why is it that when we get older, we often change our view of who we want to be?

When I was a kid, my father was a fireman. He was the first paramedic in West Dundee in the 1970s. I grew up in the early days being around firemen and fire trucks. As you have read, however, my childhood was not overly memorable for reasons I still struggle to comprehend. As my own self-reflection has progressed, I have become more understanding of who I want to be, and it has very little to do with a career or job.

Growing up, we were poor. I ate peanut butter sandwiches every day. I also attended a private Lutheran school and was surrounded by kids from affluent or upper-middle-class families. I wanted to have what they had, which, at the time, seemed to me to be money. That was the easiest answer for an elementary school-aged child: I wanted a nice house, hot meals, nice clothes, and nice cars.

Sometime in my early elementary school years, I determined that I wanted to be an accountant. Through elementary school, middle school, and high school, I continued to be surrounded by affluent people, and their influence continued to push me to make decisions based solely on the material things that money provided. During this time in my life, the answer to "Who do you want to be?" was "a person who mattered to those within my areas of influence." In my early years, the only way for me to get what I felt I needed—influence—was either to have money or to be perceived as having money. This turned me into someone I did not want to be.

Striving to fit in with a certain clique and then getting into that clique did not fulfill my quest for who I wanted to be; I just kept making bad decisions. In high school, I decided I needed more money to gain better influence over the people I wanted acceptance from. To do that, I got into drugs. My dive into drugs gave me what I thought I wanted and made me who I thought I wanted to be: a leader.

As I expanded my area of influence, I abandoned those things that I previously had a passion for: baseball, relationships, family, and more. In return for this, I acquired money, things, and fake friends who liked my things but not the person I was. These choices led to me joining the military—a 180-degree turn from who I wanted to be but a necessity for my emotional and physical development at this phase in my life.

During my time in the military, I lost touch with who I wanted to be, except I knew I wanted to be accepted. I graduated top of my class in Advanced Individual Training (AIT); then, just as I was about to receive the rewards of my accomplishments in the Army, my life changed again. This was a direct result of actions that I do not regret but wish I had better understood at the time. Regardless, my focus on being an accountant was revitalized during my time in the military.

The person I was growing into and who I aspired to be was further complicated during this time as I met my first wife, Vanessa, while I was in the military. This chance meeting resulted in my amazing daughter, Kristin, who has been an inspiration and catalyst for much of who I am today. However, the introduction of a relationship in the middle of the turmoil of being in the military, learning how to be an adult, and wanting to be an accountant created challenges in my quest for who I felt I wanted to be.

My marriage with Vanessa failed; it was doomed before it began. Nevertheless, my career as an accountant would be launched in part because of this relationship. It was my need to support my family that brought me to the man who would help define much of who I am professionally: Jack Danger.

Jack helped me to understand, better than anyone, who I wanted to be. He hired me to install a computerized accounting system at a time when computerized accounting systems were not the norm. The integration of accounting, computers, task-driven programming, and teaching people to use the systems brought into focus who I wanted to be, for the first time: a person who integrated people, process, and technology. More than that, Jack showed me that success did not come from stuff; it came from character, perseverance, and empathy.

Thus in 1988, I had learned who I wanted to be but I had not learned *how* to become who I wanted to be. It took me another eight years to grasp the true concept of applying the lessons of my life to the intentions I would create for myself. During those eight years, I learned about who I was and how where I came from contributed to that. I learned about how my decisions affected myself, my family, and those I influence. And I have since learned how to continue using the tools of self-reflection, honesty, and intention to remain true to who I want to be and who I will become.

I want to help people realize their potential in team (Individual) environments and be recognized for empowering and inspiring them. Over the years, becoming who I wanted to be evolved from chasing physical wealth, to being accepted, to learning about accounting and computers, to aiding individuals to understand how to work with computers and the people around them to make the entire company better. This process led me to creating Individual Advantages and the fulfillment of who I always really wanted to be: accepted as a leader and recognized for my contribution to something bigger than myself.

The person you want to be should not be defined by some physical job or position; it is not about the tangible things you may acquire doing that job. Instead, the person you want to be should be defined by how you proceed with your life on a daily basis and about how those actions make you feel; it's about what you end up doing in relation to the influences you have and receive.

As you read this book and begin to formulate questions that are individual to you, the answers to those questions will show you who you want to be. With these answers, you can look more clearly at who you have grown to be. My hope is that it will be easy for you to construct these questions because you know yourself best.

Who you want to be is affected by how you want to be perceived, what influences you have, and what influences you. Who you become will be defined by these things too. While your thoughts, words, and actions define who you are today, you can change who you want to be and/or reach your goals to become who you want to be by applying the lessons of this book. The journey you take will be created by your own review and application of this advice, each influencing the end result.

Key Takeaways: Who Do You Want to Be?

- Who you want to be cannot be measured by physical jobs or possessions. Who you want to be is how you show up every day to create a reality that makes you feel positive.

- Who you want to be is affected by how you want to be perceived, what influences you have, and what influences you.

- We all have influence, and understanding how you wish to influence the world around you will help you determine who you want to be.

Self-Deception

Sometimes the lies we tell ourselves are white lies: spending money, spending time, delay of action, or speed of action. We all do it, and we do it often. We all spend money we should not spend and convince ourselves that we can afford it. We've all committed to doing something in a certain amount of time and told ourselves, "I can get this done by this time." We've all said, "I don't have to start that task right now; I can finish in time." Or, "I can quickly get through this task," but you cannot. The examples are infinite. The bottom line is we lie to ourselves regularly.

So, why do we lie to ourselves? The primary reason is ego. It makes us feel better to hide behind lies and convince ourselves that picking up the pieces after we continue to do self-destructive things is easier than correcting the self-destructive behavior. *Change* may be the single most difficult word for humans, especially if change challenges the status quo—even a status quo that is destructive.

We can often justify our actions or words by playing games with specifics, use of language, or, my favorite, point of view. We can alter perception and reality by claiming *our* truth (point of view), which may or may not be true. The fact is that we all need to use context in our communication and, by doing so, we can alter perception to sway things our way through careful use of language. Although lying to yourself and others doesn't give you anything positive in return, it may provide you with the immediate gratification of being right or happy. But when you look at the bigger picture, you will find that any form of lying to yourself is only holding you back from being the best *you* that you can be.

The act of lying to ourselves to feel better is a human frailty that has no boundary. Dishonesty to ourselves and others damages our credibility and makes us inconsistent; in fact, inconsistency is itself a form of dishonesty. Our ability to trick ourselves and accept mediocrity is one way we hinder our ability to take advantage of all the opportunities that present themselves in our life.

Don't get me wrong; I still fail to adhere to my own convictions. To fail is to be human. Being honest requires hard work and patience with yourself. You will likely lie to yourself for the rest of your life, but the healthy thing to do is hold yourself accountable for your internal actions.

If you want to be honest with yourself, first ask why you lie in the first place. What is motivating you to be dishonest with yourself and then with others? What is it that needs to be achieved? My motivation was wanting to be accepted. Since I found out early that perception is reality, it's easy to create a false perception. What would happen if you cleared the smoke, smashed the mirrors, and were just you?

For some, being *you* may be gregarious, high-profile, and boisterous. René is the most friendly and outgoing person I have ever known. When René walks into a room, she can steal the show; her enthusiasm and pure happiness are almost overpowering—at times, I feel like a bump on a log. René is also naturally beautiful; she is blessed with that rare combination of inner and outer beauty that everyone sees and feels.

However, there are some people who see René and think, "That cannot be her true self; this must be an act." Those of us who know her know that this is the real René; there is no wavering in her personality nor in how she presents herself to the world. The "naysayers" learn this pretty fast. (Pun intended: I call René "Nay.")

I've often wondered how René came to be this beautiful person. Where does this inner beauty come from? Recently, René shared with me that she is terrified by new situations. They make her uncomfortable and create a high level of anxiety. I was floored by this information. I took some time to think about it and wondered: could it be that René has been faking who she is all this time?

Reflecting on over 30 years together, I knew the answer was no; René is as honest about herself as she is with others. Her anxiety just turbocharges her friendliness and ability to warm up a relationship. René is who she is and does not put on airs or have a pretentious bone in her body. She shields her anxiety, yes, but in doing so, she has not created a false persona or developed traits that negatively affect others. It *enhances* her foundational personality without altering it.

As for me, that kind of anxiety management and self-confidence took half a lifetime to acquire. I would often justify my behavior in my own mind, lying to myself along the way. I bought cars I should not have bought, wore clothes that gave off a certain look, and participated in functions that I despised but embraced as if they were a normal part of my life, all to provide the world with a perception that I was affluent. What I did not realize is that many people liked me for who I was without those actions, and I would have more true friends today had I understood these acts of self-deception much sooner.

In the end, you need to figure out for yourself what is real and what is not. As you begin to slow down and self-reflect, your focus will become clearer, and you will be able to distinguish between the things that provide you with a false image and a true image. Whatever choice you make, if you're *honest* about the choice, it will probably support who you ultimately want to be.

Key Takeaways: Self-Deception

- We lie to ourselves because it makes us feel good to hide behind the lies and convince ourselves of a false reality.

- We often want our lies to be truth, and the ultimate self-deception is living through the lies as truth.

- Being honest requires hard work and patience. Honesty can be painful for us *and* for others.

Intuition

Throughout your life, opportunities will arise for you. The more you know yourself and slow down, the more advantages you will create that provide opportunities. You may be asking, "How does self-reflection and slowing down work? How do I know if an opportunity is the right opportunity? Are there ways to know if it is not the right one?" I think there are, and the first thing you need to do is listen to your intuition (or what some may call your "gut feeling" or "instinct").

One way to accurately listen to your intuition is to listen to your emotions. Sometimes our emotions can block our ability to be mindful, meaning we need to challenge opportunities that are a result of pure emotion. Both positive and negative emotions can interfere with our ability to create advantages in our decisions or actions. For example, reactive tendencies often eliminate opportunity by alienating us from people or opportunities that might otherwise provide additional benefits to us. A good place to start is to ask yourself the following: "What is fueling the emotion, and how may that emotion influence my ability to make sound decisions?"

Self-reflection is a good tool when this occurs because you may discover a secret agenda buried in your mind that conflicts with your current life, or worse, is something that you should not be doing. This may be the most difficult to differentiate, but let's look at my own history of emotional decisions that have altered or delayed my purpose in life so far.

Baseball will be the crux of my lesson here. I have previously mentioned my love for baseball. I so loved the game that at 28, I embarked on a quest to play Major League Baseball—despite my age and the fact that I had not been playing at any professional competitive level. At the time, I had been married for under two years, and my business was young but stable. René was pregnant with Mary, and I was not in the best shape of my life. So, why did I do this? Ego.

I was a good baseball player as a kid. I had a friend who was drafted into MLB right out of high school. My business provided me with an opportunity to work with baseball players and teams, giving me the idea that maybe I could play. So, I tried. During my time in Florida playing in Spring Training Tryouts for the Houston Astros, I was injured. I had to go to the hospital and ended up in a sling, forcing me to pull out of the tryouts. I had good memories and some very cool experiences, but I wasn't ready to give up on baseball.

As soon as we got back to Colorado, I began looking to play ball on a competitive team. I landed in a local semi-pro league and, with my training to try out at MLB camps, was good enough to make the All-Star team in the league. At this time, MLB was going through some issues—a strike was looming—and I felt like I had a shot at playing as a scab player. (Scab is the common, usually unflattering, term for a person who crosses the picket line of protesting union workers.) However, life had different plans for me. I was in a car accident, hit by a drunk driver, and both of my wrists were so severely injured that I needed three operations.

Now, you'd think I would be done after these events, but I love baseball. A couple years later, I had another opportunity. I had a friend who played on a competitive baseball team. At the time, I was 34, and our companies were doing pretty well. Henry was a baby and Mary was six; my infatuation with golf after moving onto a golf course was waning. I joined the team and immediately had a position; my ability to play well came back quickly, and I was identified as one of the top players. Again, I was nominated to play on the All-Star team. Then, just as I felt I was hitting my stride, something happened; my thumb was crushed to the point where my thumb bone was broken into over eight pieces.

Did this incident give me pause? Do you think I slowed down or reflected on my history in baseball? Nope. When we moved to Oregon, there was another team. This team was ranked second in the United States in its league, and I would be the oldest player by over 14 years but I started. This time I made it through about two-thirds of the season before my left rotator cuff and bicep muscle tore; then I was done.

At this time, I did one of my self-reflections and saw clearly that professional sports, specifically baseball, were not meant to be in my life. Looking back over my timeline, I could trace this issue back to 1978, when I moved from Illinois to California for the first time. One of the main reasons I decided to move was to get away from the issues I was having with baseball in Illinois. Those issues continued to show themselves through high school and then into my adult life, over and over. Unfortunately, my ego, emotions, and going too fast got in the way of me realizing that baseball was not meant to be in my life; that realization took over 20 years.

The conclusion of my attempt to stay connected to baseball happened in 2016. I was afforded the opportunity to coach at my original high school, where I played in ninth grade. As a sophomore, Henry was playing on the team and I was asked to help—a dream for me. Within eight weeks of agreeing, I threw out my right rotator cuff and ended up with another surgery. Even after learning my lesson to not play, I hadn't connected the dots to understand I was not supposed to be involved in baseball at all, ever.

Life gives us signs that our intuition usually analyzes correctly, but only when we slow down and pay attention. Now, I'm not saying that every bad thing that happens is a sign not to do something. But if you are trying to do something, and you are repeatedly given a sign that it's not the right thing for you, like me and baseball, you need to pay attention. This is where slowing down and being honest with yourself can come into play. Today I know that I get just as much enjoyment watching baseball as I do participating. My need to participate was fueled by my need to be in control and stemmed from what I perceived as a position of influence. Now I know I could have provided more positive moments in my life (and the lives of others) had I yielded sooner, slowed down, and listened to my intuition.

When challenges are presented, pause to ask yourself why you are being challenged. What is the challenge? Under what context is it being provided? It's normal to struggle with reaching your goals. Things that come easily should be reflected on just as much as things that come with difficulty. The more thought and planning you put into your life decisions, the more fluid those decisions will appear. However, we can get into a comfortable focus in those things that we feel we know well; this allows part of our ego to take over, potentially creating struggles and obstacles in our path due to our own arrogance, insecurity, difficulty following through, ignorance, or stupidity.

Regardless of whether your path is positive or negative, you must understand that path and how you got there before you can move forward honestly and with a positive influence. Understanding where we are in the present offers the clarity we all need to progress.

Key Takeaways: Intuition

- Reactive tendencies can alienate you from opportunity, so challenge your emotions when they are sudden, negative, and reactionary.

- Slow down and pay attention to the signs life gives you. They are always there!

- You should reflect on things that come easily just as much as things that come with difficulty.

- Trust your intuition, even if it is a small voice inside you. Your intuition is usually right and will steer you onto the right path.

Clarity

Recollection is about clarity, about who you are and, eventually, about your purpose here in this life. We all have a purpose, and by gaining clarity about your past, you have a better chance at understanding and accepting that purpose. Now, this is not about settling. I believe that each and every person has a specific purpose. That includes being the best we can be as individuals and giving something that enhances the Individuals (teams) we influence—and we all have influence.

I've written about my initial recollection and how some follow-up recollections have clarified some issues in my life. However, baseball is not where I will leave this lesson. My life path has led me to a point where I have the foundation, experience, and knowledge to share with the world why individual influence is neither singular nor plural; it has been and will always be cyclical and all-encompassing. It is part of every single human on Earth, in the past, present, and future.

In the early days of IA, I felt like I needed a foundation for my concepts. At first, I had no idea where to begin. Up until 1996, I had been primarily an IT/accounting guy installing computerized accounting systems and not really paying specific attention to my past or how it influenced me. My lessons about business processes and the complexities of human interaction in the workplace were lost in the speed of doing business in the mid-1990s. My focus was on making money, speeding up the workplace, and making it more efficient.

Up until 1995, I had not traveled much. Beginning in 1996, I was flying all over the world, and by 1999, those travels had increased to over 100,000 miles a year. At that same time, we built a home, Mary entered kindergarten, and IA had taken shape. I was also fully committed to my doctoral studies and doing a lot of research on human interaction between workers and technology. Through this research, I kept reflecting on the parallels in my life, and each time, I dove as deep as my memory would allow.

One of the issues I struggled with was my connection to my parents. If we are shaped by our past, what kind of parent and what kind of leader would I be? As you have read, my childhood was chaotic and, upon further recollection, unstructured until eighth grade. During a self-reflection in 1999, I recalled the structure introduced to me by my stepparents, Bill and Michele. Both of them came into my life at about the same time and brought a certain amount of structure that neither my sister nor I had up to that point. In fact, I cannot recall any structure whatsoever, to the point that one of my memories is downright frightening.

I must have been in third or fourth grade, and it was fall. At the time, we lived right next door to Highlands Elementary School (the public elementary school in West Dundee), but my sister and I attended Immanuel (the private Lutheran school). We were not generally accepted by the kids in the neighborhood; in fact, I was bullied a lot. One day, my sister and I were sitting in the house alone (mind you, she is three years younger than me). As the kids from Highlands walked by, I spied them through the scope of my father's 30.06 deer rifle. I don't recall where my parents were, but I do recall the feelings of that time—emptiness and loneliness. Unfortunately, even at that age, we were left to our own devices.

You may ask why this story resonates in my mind about lack of structure. My parents were very young and, I suspect, did not realize what my sister and I were enduring. What resonated with me was the ridicule and bullying we both received from the kids who walked by our home every day. I could not defend my sister against everyone who bullied her, and I lacked the confidence to stand up to those who bullied me. Struggling to make ends meet, raise a young family, and provide a private education, my young parents had no clue what my sister or I were going through, and they could not really protect us. While I do not blame my parents individually, I do realize that they did not understand at the time that the lack of parental structure provided me with the idea of picking up a rifle to scope out the kids who tormented us. I imagined I could ward them off from the safety of my living room.

As I recall this story, I am struck by the news of recent school shootings; could I have been one of those shooters? What signs are being missed by parents, teachers, and other people of influence that might help to resolve the demons created by the actions of human against human? What demons did this event and those that led to me pointing a rifle at children, as a child, survive into my adult life? I know that, to this day, I am protective of my sister and anyone else who is bullied or picked on. I always root for the underdog. I can adapt, and have adapted, to almost any situation; I have a tremendous sense of situational awareness when presented with a new environment or changes to my current environment. I accept people, good and bad, for who they are at the time and believe that each person can be better. Most of all, my ability to empathize has been the single biggest benefit of this event. In fact, my empathy and ability to support others to do the same may be one of the biggest influencers in my life.

Key Takeaways: Clarity

- All humans have influence.
- We all have a purpose, and by gaining clarity about your past, you have a better chance at understanding and accepting that purpose.
- When we understand our purpose, our influence becomes focused.
- We are all a byproduct of previous influence, up to and including the present moment.

Who Am I? Reflection

Well, our journey together is just beginning. So far, we have explored who we are and how who we are forms the building blocks of our foundation. We should have a glimpse of what we face within ourselves at this point; that glimpse is part of our foundation. Keep these realizations at the top of your mind as we continue to dive deeper into what makes you an individual.

Chapter 5

Foundation

"When the roots
are deep, there is
no reason to fear
the wind."
—African Proverb

Being self-aware is a cornerstone of your foundation. Therefore, knowing who you are today and how your past has influenced you should never again be neglected. We are all products of our environment, which includes our family, friends, community, culture, socioeconomic status, education, religion, beliefs, political influences, career, and overall day-to-day life experiences. These elements, and more, are your foundation. Your foundation is where you came from—your experiences combined with your perception of those experiences. Your foundation is made up of everyone who has influenced you up to this point in your life and how you influence the world based on everything you have been through. Your foundation is what makes you a "we"! Recognizing your foundation allows you to understand yourself, and when you understand yourself, you can more easily control yourself and grow.

I have heard many people say, "I want to forget the past." I personally don't think that's healthy. The past offers you an opportunity to ensure you do not repeat mistakes. Being aware of how your past is manifested in your present will help you to refine your actions in the future. Understanding how we can be a positive influence, and then being that positive influence despite a dark and traumatic past, is the ultimate form of mental endurance, training, and thinking. In fact, resilience to the negative influences of the world is how we can all become more present, aware, and positive.

For example, if one of your earliest memories is getting into a car accident, you may experience a twinge of anxiety every time you get into a car, or you might not drive at all, preferring to bike or use public transportation should that be available to you. Or you may have worked in a toxic environment where you had a leader or co-worker who left a negative impression on working with certain types of individuals or in a certain environment. You may have been exposed to a work culture that tolerated this negative behavior, which may influence how you behave or respond to work relationships and environments in the present. The experiences that create your foundation shape your current reality and how you interact with the world today. By understanding where you come from and what you have experienced, you can pave the way for where you are going, work on that within yourself you deem worthy, and discover your unique positive influence.

To discover your foundation, you must set aside or reconcile your ego and be honest with yourself about who you are, inside and out. Your foundation may have cracks, as many of ours do; you may have habits and character flaws that you want to dispose of or change, but how can you shore up your foundation if you don't first learn what it's made of? To change anything, you must first understand its true nature. Otherwise, you are likely only temporarily altering that which influences you while allowing for what you wish to change to remain prevalent. To be better for yourself and those you influence, you must gaze into your internal mirror and find your foundation.

Self-Awareness

Why, you might ask, would we want to dive so deep into our past to discuss our psychological foundation in a book about leadership? Because your foundation as a leader supports you, your family, and the people you influence every day through your thoughts, words, and actions. The load you put on your personal foundation will change throughout your life, and if you're not prepared to recognize the flaws (weak points) when they appear and shore them up, you *and* those you influence can be negatively affected. This is where the importance of self-awareness, self-discovery, and self-exploration comes into play.

For the purpose of this section, we will define self-awareness as encompassing self-discovery and self-exploration, as these two actions lead one to be more self-aware. Self-awareness, in its simplest terms, is being aware of your mind; it's understanding why you do the things you do and think the way you think. In part, it encompasses mindfulness, which is a non-judgmental exploration of your thought processes to better understand how your mind shapes who you are and your perception of the world. You'll start by exploring your mind by remaining curious rather than judgmental, which will lead to discovery, which then leads to awareness of self.

This "awareness of self" comes with an understanding that we are not wholly individual, meaning we are a culmination of all that influences us. Self begins with understanding "I," knowing "I" is important but that "I" is never only singular for you or for anyone. We are an "I" and a "we" at all times; we are a "we" because of those who have shaped us and influenced us through experiences.

With this understanding, we can now know how important we (I) are and why being our best self is so important not only for us but for all who we influence. Thus, self-awareness and recognition of our role as part of a "we" helps us be our most positive influence.

Understanding how your past has affected who you are in this moment is critical to moving forward. For those of us who are happy with where we are today, refining or polishing our present self can also be aided by self-awareness. For those of us who have issues we wish to resolve, self-awareness can help us overcome the mental barriers holding us back. Many of us carry emotional baggage, memories that stir emotions that affect the way we communicate with ourselves and others. When emotions dictate how we communicate, how we communicate becomes ineffective and is often destructive to our foundation.

Take my life as an example here: I hate all surprises. Any action that can be deemed a surprise has the potential to instill in me a negative emotion rapidly. One day, I had to ask myself, "Why? How is it that I can be calm, focused, and intentional, and with a single surprise have my entire day derailed?"

Upon reflection, there are a few defining moments in my childhood that led me to the source of my dislike of surprises. The first moment is my move in the fourth grade from West Dundee (Immanuel Lutheran) to Wood Dale (Zion Lutheran). Moving is hard for any child; learning about the move one day before it happens is *traumatic*. I was already an angry child; I was surrounded by people who seemed to have stability—like my classmates—and my only constant, attending school, was suddenly upended. My life timeline shows clear signs of my uneasiness about change that stems from moving, and a common factor is that each of my subsequent moves was also a surprise to me. Each surprise move contributed to my next phase of needing control. I needed to "fix" my instability.

When I unexpectedly moved to California at the end of seventh grade, I forced myself to make a decision in light of my instability: I moved back to Illinois before eighth grade. My eighth- and ninth-grade school years were stable but marked by the surprise of my father marrying a woman who was only seven years older than me. That event never evolved into a good experience for me, and in order to prevent further surprises, I moved back to California right before tenth grade.

My chaotic decision-making was my attempt to assert some control and avoid future surprises; these decisions were primarily made out of rash determination instead of patience or perseverance in situations that were uncomfortable for me at the time. I altered my future to remain in control. Sometime after meeting René, this changed for me. René became an anchor that allowed me to explore more challenging decisions, since being in a relationship with her continued to ground me mentally and physically. Even though I recognize my decision-making pattern today, the change from chaotic, impulsive decision-making to thoughtful, more controlled, and coordinated decision-making was not a conscious change on my part. In fact, I did not realize this pattern until the early 2000s.

One of the most memorable and unpleasant surprises for me was my 30th birthday party (when I seriously started to consider why I hated surprises so much). It was 1996, and professionally, I was in transition. IA had just become a legal entity. The idea behind IA was new, and I was mentally preoccupied. I had just sold our accounting system implementation business, was working for the company that bought it, and began to travel more frequently. One day, I came home to a house full of people—a surprise party. The first person I saw was a classmate from Thousand Oaks High School who had never been a close friend, and to see him intensified the discomfort of surprise.

You'd think such an event with family and friends would be good, but no. Our home was a work in process, as we purchased it as a fixer-upper, and it was nowhere near complete. I was also a work in process—I was turning 30, I had just sold our first company on top of just coming through multiple surgeries due to a car crash, and I was dealing with new bosses and a new work environment. And, of course, our marriage was a work in process with a new child. Chaos comes in many ways, and when your life is a work in process as mine was at this time, a surprise party took the normal chaos of my life and created one of the worst events in my life.

To this day, I still don't like surprises of any kind, good or bad. However, after exploring and discovering the reasons behind my intense dislike of surprises, this awareness has become more important as my responsibility to others has increased and, now, my reaction to surprises is less tumultuous. I channel my emotion into the proper place to not create surprise moments for others created by *my* actions. By this I mean that I work to not show negative emotions to those who surprise me; these negative emotions can often be a surprise to others. Believe me, some people don't take too kindly when your reaction to surprise events that are meant to be positive is markedly negative.

When you have reactions that are immediate, such as negative emotions, and you want to control them or stop them from happening, you need to become more self-aware. Begin your process with curiosity and explore your past to look for reasons why you may feel or think this way in the present. You will need to remain honest with yourself in order to discover the true nature of your foundation. Through self-discovery, you will become more aware. However, if you wish to change things that are part of you naturally, you are going to need to work to create a new habit that defines the person you want to be.

Key Takeaways: Self-Awareness

- Self-exploration and self-discovery are the beginning of the self-awareness process. Explore, discover, and become aware of your own mind.

- When engaged in the process of becoming self-aware, abandon judgment and choose curiosity.

- When emotions dictate how you communicate, how you communicate becomes ineffective and is often destructive to your foundation.

Habits

We all have habits, good and bad. Habits are the automatic and repetitive actions that will ultimately define you and contribute greatly to your ability to succeed, fail, fit in, and be content. Even simple habits that seem personal to us, and don't seem to have a direct influence on others, can actually prove to have a dramatic effect.

There are a few habits with a physical aspect that everyone can relate to in one way or another: biting nails, skin picking, and hair-pulling. These are well-studied and are classified as Body-Focused Repetitive Behaviors (BFRB). René and I both bite our nails, and I also pick the skin on my fingers. Too much information, right? This is a habit that has no literal impact on a third party. The fact that my nails are short and some skin is picked away has no bearing on my ability to be a good consultant. However, the unsightly appearance can be off-putting to people who judge others critically for such habits; thus, it *could* have a direct effect that is unintended or even undeserved.

Only one of our children is a nail-biter, so does this habit have a genetic component, or is it a learned trait based on observation? How do you overcome these habits in support of creating more advantages for yourself? Though we explore this in a later section, we encourage you to ponder how these questions apply to you as a unique individual, as well as some habits in your life that can be deemed positive or negative (as defined by you). Another common habit is the use of cultural, generational, or societal phrases or words. When I met René, she used the word "whatnot" all the time when speaking; however, she did not use the word when writing. Why is this?

Understanding habits can help us solve those things in our life we wish to change. Our habits, whether genetic or learned, are important to define so we can approach changing them with a positive mindset. The key here is that *we* define what we would like to change. For example, we all know smoking is bad for us, but some don't value health or feel they need to stop. That is for them to decide. However, if you make a choice to stop smoking, you can build a healthier habit to replace it. So, if we can identify a habit we dislike and work to change it, we can make progress and create new advantages for ourselves. On the other hand, if we observe a behavior we'd like to develop in ourselves, we can arrange to spend the time and effort to repeat the task to the point that it becomes habitual. Habits can be used to overcome certain addictions, which are really just dependent habits in the end.

Do something consistently for three to six weeks, and it will likely become a habit. There are exceptions to this, but generally speaking, it holds true. The hard part, however, will be holding yourself accountable to sticking to what is needed to keep going as your life changes and adapts to the new action. This applies to almost anything. Want to start working out at a certain time on certain days? Find a way to work out on those days for three to six weeks without any interruption, and your chances of doing it consistently in the future will be very high. I used this trick to create the habit of reading trade rags, as I mentioned earlier. I needed a way to stay well-read on the various industries that I consult for, and the amount and variety of information I needed to know were growing so fast that unless I found a way to keep up, I was at risk of becoming irrelevant. So, I began making time to read them until it became a habit for me. Now I never miss an issue.

Take a moment to identify the unique habits of the people around you (which could also be called patterns). Your family, friends, and peers all have certain patterns that influence you, and you have patterns that influence them. As stated, patterns are synonymous with habits, and it's important to understand them as part of your self-awareness process. If you are mimicking the actions of others—that is, following a pattern—those actions will eventually become your habit regardless of whether you continue to be around the person you picked it up from, and you may, in turn, influence others to acquire the same pattern (habits).

In my business, I often work with businesses that don't have documented policies and procedures; instead, they have habits or patterns. These patterns are the way they do things to keep the company going, but they are not written down or documented—it's just "the way they do it." When new people come into the organization and mimic what others are doing, their actions become new habits. These patterns may or may not be efficient or healthy for the business or for individuals, yet they do them over and over, repeating even the most difficult and frustrating tasks because "it's the way it's always been done."

This is the trap that habits can spring on us. We get so comfortable with what we are doing that we are numb to its effects. This is why examining our habits and determining if they are healthy or unhealthy for us is imperative. Should you want to build new habits in place of old ones, you must define what that new habit is and stick to it for a minimum of three weeks before it will start to become a habit. By identifying habits or patterns, you can correctly put them into perspective and use them to effect change and create more advantages. Keep track of your progress using a journal, grid tracker, or app on your phone (or any other way that will help you document and track your progress). Part of your influence will stem from the effects of your habits, good and bad, which will influence your character and personality.

Key Takeaways: Habits

- By understanding your habits, you can begin to solve some of the issues in your life by replacing habits that you deem negative with more positive ones.

- Working to replace negative habits with positive habits can create new opportunities and advantages.

- Habits are a lot like comfortable focus; you can become numb to them. Depending on the habit, this can affect your character and personality. Therefore, you must know your habits.

Character

Your character is the culmination of your behavior in all aspects and is generally measured by how you influence others. Your character often emerges in how you present yourself in rare and extreme circumstances, forcing you to act quickly without thought. It is also part of your foundation; for example, how you communicate and how others understand your communication may be driven by your character traits and enhanced by your personality. Character can often take time to reveal itself, as it is primarily based on a person's internal beliefs and values, while judging personality is easier and faster to categorize when you meet someone for the first time.

While character matters in almost all you do, as an innate part of who you are, personality is defined by how you present yourself to others. However, different facets of your personality can come out in different situations while character takes time to reveal. In this way, personality can be faked or masked for situational influence, whereas character is much harder to fake. A person's character can be impugned or enhanced but not *determined* by someone's personality; you cannot truly know someone's character by how they dress or present themselves visually.

Personality is your outward visible self, often influenced by ego, and can be altered at a whim. Personality and character are both influenced by your inner self; however, how people label you (your personality) may not even be who you truly are, as it can mask your flaws and even fool people into believing your character is something it is not. Character, however, is proven one positive or negative action at a time, and it is often revealed when an individual is caught off-guard.

You can define or identify someone's personality as serious, shy, lazy, or outgoing (to name just a few). These personality traits can lead to a character assessment; for example, a serious person may be deemed to have good character because they appear to be sincere and approach things thoughtfully. However, another serious person may be deemed to have a questionable character because the person appears to be overly direct or intrusive. Similarly, a shy person may be deemed to have an arrogant or snobbish character.

One of the biggest ways to differentiate between personality and character is over time. One can influence emotion quickly with personality, but revealing character can take time. For example, knowing if someone is honest—a character trait—doesn't automatically denote understanding how that person reacts to issues that are based on honesty or a lack thereof, based on their personality; they may react negatively or aggressively, but that has nothing to do with their honest character. Being kind or virtuous can require time to measure, while personality traits are something that can be evaluated almost immediately.

Let's look at a common example we can all relate to. Say you are in a good mood and you encounter someone who is also in a good mood. You may have a positive conversation that leaves you both feeling fond of each other. This conversation may easily demonstrate your personality as you feel positive. If you continue building a relationship with this person, you will begin to notice their character traits emerge. Are they always positive and upbeat, or do they start to become more negative and cynical as you get to know them? The longer you know someone, the easier it is to identify their personality traits (what they show you when they are feeling good or want to make a good impression) and their character traits (the things that influence their most natural and innate behaviors/responses).

Another example: you have a new team member who has historically been very positive and upbeat. One day, you go into work not feeling as happy as usual, and perhaps you are less talkative due to feeling sad, anxious, or even angry. You may have determined that this new team member has a kind personality, but that determination is made based on positive conversations you've had in this short period of time. Now, this new team member can treat you a few different ways if you aren't quite feeling yourself, and how they treat you when you're experiencing natural human emotions will be a determining factor in their character. Do they ask you if you are okay and what is wrong? Do they reflect your mood back to you and take it personally? Do they try to give you space? Character can be evoked from someone in circumstances that don't match past events and present a chance for them to behave differently.

Let's further these examples with a real-life story. I am often told that I am too direct (a personality trait). I also work very hard to be honest (a character trait) in all I do because I've found that being dishonest is one of the worst things you can be to anyone, including yourself. Honesty is a character trait that almost all people would love to be known for; even liars strive to be thought of as honest. However, honesty will someday put you in a position to answer a question or tell someone something that will be taken negatively. As mentioned, character traits can be presented in extreme circumstances.

Thus, being honest can sometimes put you in an awkward position. I have some dramatic examples of being honest that, on the surface, appear mean-spirited. Some issues are every day and even commonsense, but people looking in from the outside still perceive honesty as cruel. Below is one such example.

We once had an IT consultant who had horrible halitosis, so bad that being around him was like being around a sewer. I did not work with this person; in fact, I did not hire him and cannot recall being within 30 feet of him in the first 3 months he worked for us. We began to notice that other consultants shied away from working with him, so I asked our team questions, but none shared anything with me. One day, one of my clients called and said he had a complaint about one of our consultants. That complaint was lodged by his staff, who said our consultant had a hygiene issue.

I immediately called his project manager, told them that we had received a complaint about this person's hygiene, and asked the project manager to please discuss it with him. The reply I received was unacceptable because it forced me to handle a situation that is commonsense and, quite frankly, should not be something that goes on for three months.

I sat the consultant down and almost immediately detected the issue: poor oral hygiene. The thing is that he had white teeth, so the issue wasn't apparent by his looks. The issue was much larger than just bad breath. When confronted, the consultant admitted that he had been aware of the issue for some time. He said he went through bottles of mouthwash and brushed his teeth many times a day. Amazingly, none of the people he worked with at our company had said a word to him.

The issue was compounded by the fact this consultant was very good at what he did. His input was requested by his teammates and our clients. The other issue is that he knew he was in demand and thought his superficial approach was enough; as smart as he was, he refused to address the root cause and tried to cover it up with mouthwash and vigorous brushing. This is an issue of arrogant character coupled with an oblivious personality.

After hearing that he had gone to superficial lengths but not really addressed the root cause of the issue, I relieved him of his work duties until he sought out professional help. He was in disbelief that I would put him on unpaid leave, but his issue was that severe. I told him that he was not being penalized for a physical issue but for a character issue by not addressing the fact that his halitosis was causing others tremendous discomfort and also affecting the company's reputation. His inability to identify that he had a bigger issue concerned me on more than a few levels. What other issues might this person have bad judgment on?

Acceptance of things that are not generally accepted is a character issue; it's a form of ego and arrogance. For this consultant to think that his mind was so great that people should look past and accept his horrible bad breath is a character flaw. We see this time and again; people expect others to accept bad behavior because they think they are special in some way. There are ways to damage your character other than simply connecting the physical self to the mental self.

Working in my industry, I have had to be honest with people about many uncomfortable things. I am sure many people would shy away from most of the things I have had to be honest about. As in my previous example, nobody that I worked with came forward and was honest about this consultant's hygiene issue; even when I asked questions, nobody said anything. Honesty isn't always about bringing people happy news. It's about having enough respect for the other human being to lay it all on the line for them. Sometimes this kind of honesty can get you labeled as an asshole. For me, being labeled as dishonest is a far worse punishment. Being labeled as dishonest will stick with a person; even if the person rebuilds a reputation for speaking the truth, the stigma of being dishonest can rear its ugly head.

Another issue with character is that it can be called into question just by the company you keep or the profession you're in. For example, being a politician carries inherent questions from people who oppose or do not share your political affiliation. Democrats question Republicans and vice versa. Similarly, being an attorney or used car salesperson often comes with challenges to your character as part of long-standing generalizations. When we have long-standing generalizations, we begin to form bias, which can be unconscious, subconscious, or conscious. (We discuss bias in more detail in a future chapter.) In all aspects of our bias, we have the potential to challenge our influence and become more self-aware.

Personality can change in a moment; we may appear happy or sad with a simple change in how an interaction happens. However, changing our impression of a person's character takes time, sometimes months or even years. This is particularly difficult when our impression of character is influenced by our biases. Understanding that perception is reality, we must remain mindful of the perception we create for ourselves in others' realities. Their reality of you is a combination of your personality, character, and potentially their own biases, which are determined over time and through diverse events by your words and actions.

Key Takeaways: Character

- Measuring character takes time while measuring personality can be done either instantaneously or over time.

- Honesty, an important character trait, is about having enough respect for the other person to lay it all on the line for them.

- Your character may be called into question depending on the people you hang around, the industry you're in, or even your political affiliation.

- People can spend a lifetime developing their character, but some can destroy your character in a moment; be mindful of your influence.

Perception Is Reality

Having a questionable character can cause a lot of difficulties for a person. Being labeled as untrustworthy, dishonest, selfish, narcissistic, or spiteful can stay with you for a long time. However, identifying a character flaw and alleviating that flaw are both challenging. We have discussed that self-assessment can be difficult, and being honest about character issues can prove to be the most difficult. Often, we justify our actions that damage our character, forgetting that perception of action and result goes beyond our own definition.

We moved to Klamath Falls, Oregon, in 2005. Though the move there was easy for me, it was difficult for my family. René was born and raised in Colorado, and her entire social world was there. Henry was four, so he had not established himself in school or with a large number of friends. Mary, however, was entering sixth grade and had established friendships at a critical time in a young girl's life.

My goal in moving was to spend more time with my family. As a consultant, I traveled a lot and had missed most of my children's lives due to work and travel. Moving to Oregon was an opportunity to change that. My primary goal in 2005 was working with a client who had contracted me to move to Oregon and personally oversee their business operations. Meanwhile, IA kept running in the background and required very little of my time.

As an international consultant moving from Denver to Klamath Falls, I brought with me a perspective of business and leadership that was dramatically different from what a small, rural mountain community was used to. Employee, vendor, and customer relationships were not similar to those you might see in urban or suburban areas.

Early on, some of my character traits became a challenge to some. My direct and up-front way of discussing issues caused some problems. I would (and continue to) engage people in direct communication about any issue we are facing. I speak honestly about an issue, and I do so without emotion. That style of management quickly got labeled me as an asshole.

Vendors did not like that I would challenge them. There was a food vendor who had done business with the company for 5 years, who probably had 75 percent of the wholesale food business in town with restaurants. He was well-known, a local who had grown up in the area and had a lot of influence.

One of the first things I did upon taking over day-to-day operations was to reconcile our purchasing programs and validate our vendor performance and pricing. Food cost was a major concern to me, as it was a double-digit percentage higher than it should've been. Inventory and portion controls did not seem to move the needle more than a couple of percentage points over the first few inventory reviews and financial cycles, so I revisited our vendor pricing.

I was visited early in the process by this vendor and challenged as to why I would question his pricing. I explained to him that our cost numbers were higher than they should be and that it was not due to portion or inventory control issues, which left us with the original cost of food. The relationship with this vendor ended.

No more than five months later, my character would be challenged. During my initial time in the position, a number of local restaurant owners learned that I was not an employee of the company I was working for but a management consultant. Later, most owners learned that I actually had equity in the company, changing my social status from an "outsider manager" to a "local business owner," which opened doors of communication.

One of the first things I offered to these business owners was what we commonly call "low hanging fruit." I told them they should price shop their food vendor. It took one month for my character to be challenged by the status quo in Klamath Falls. I was approached by more than a few who accused me of all sorts of bad things, including price-fixing, unethical business practices, home-wrecking (how this one spiraled out, I will never know), and being against local business. Eventually, these turned into accusations of being a liar, cheater, and all-around bad guy. To reiterate my point, all I did was change food vendors to save my company money.

Did you ever play the Telephone Game as a kid? Tell one person a story, and when that person tells the story to the next one, the following iteration of the story will be slightly different. Two things happened immediately as a result of this series of character assassinations: Our food service declined, and I decided that all our local vendors needed to be challenged.

Meanwhile, my reputation continued to be attacked. In fact, up to this day, you can still find a large number of business people who will tell you that I'm an asshole. Ask them to give you a specific reason, and not one can objectively do so. But perception is reality. I even began to think of myself as an asshole and wore the term like a badge of honor while living in Klamath Falls. However, this was to be yet another lesson for me, and it took getting to the root of the issue to learn how it would affect my life.

Suffice it to say, the business began making money in food operations and all other operations as well. We went on to build a hotel, and during that process, I reinforced with a number of local businesspeople the idea that I was—in their mind—an asshole, and they perpetuated that within their spheres of influence. The act of embracing my new label severely damaged my reputation. It affected my partners, my family, and my friends. Again, perception is reality, and as I reinforced this label, my character as an asshole was perceived as such by all who did not know me well.

What is missing from perception, however, is context. Ever heard that there are three sides to every story? People who heard from the food vendor only heard his side of the story and did not understand the context. I did not help the situation when people would approach me and say, "I heard you're a pretty tough businessman, kind of an ass." To which I would say, "Yep, that's me."

My reality is that I want everyone to succeed. I had nothing personal against that food salesman, but his prices were too high for my business. In fact, this label followed me on numerous occasions in Klamath Falls for challenging people's prices or lack of customer service. I was labeled a lot of things based on initial perceptions; all of the labels challenged my character.

I am guilty of things that damage character. In my life, I have lied, cheated, and stolen. Those decisions do not reflect my character today, and anyone who labels me that way is lost. I am often empathetic with myself, and I think that once you can be empathetic with yourself, your character will improve.

Key Takeaways: Perception Is Reality

- Your perception is your reality, but other people's perception is their reality. Be mindful of who you are or who you are perceived to be.

- Your influence is part of the perception equation; people perceive based on the influences in their life.

- Never discount the power of context and the influence it has on perceptions.

Empathy

Empathy is the ability to recognize, categorize, and understand the emotions another person is feeling and then respond in a way that makes the experience comforting for all parties. It may also involve feeling the emotions another person is feeling. Generally, empathy is a positive influence for the giver and receiver. The act of empathy can be carried out regardless of whether you created the emotions another person is experiencing or not; you can empathize with those who are experiencing something you didn't cause, and you can empathize with those who are experiencing something as a direct result of your words or actions. Demonstrating empathy for others doesn't require having a previously established relationship with them. Empathy does not always require a tremendous amount of personal or emotional investment; generally, it simply requires the giver of empathy to be invested in a positive experience with others.

To give an example of one of my public displays of empathy, I provide the following. When I or someone I influence makes a character mistake, I will challenge myself or that person to rectify the issue. I am involved in an association, IKECA (International Kitchen Exhaust Cleaning Association). One of our companies (Omni Containment Systems) is a manufacturing company and sells to the primary members of this organization. Our company has a tremendous amount of influence in the market, and I have been representing this company at IKECA since 2009.

About eight years ago, I began teaching business and leadership sessions at IKECA in the name of Individual Advantages. I wanted to bring to IKECA some of the lessons we teach our clients around the world. My personal influence at IKECA has grown, and my character is as good as anyone with the same record of membership in the organization.

Omni has a competitor that is also very involved at IKECA. This competitor is a good company that is owned by a larger company and provides very similar products to the kitchen exhaust cleaning (KEC) market. About seven years ago, Omni decided to develop a product that could be used in the competitor's system. That system is not patented, so our development was within the normal scope of business. Omni had just finished defending a patent violation on one of our products, and that issue was public, so the company position and my position on intellectual property of any kind was visible and understood by all.

My session with the IKECA membership that day was about leadership. About five minutes before my presentation, the president of the competitor approached me with a piece of paper in his hand. On that paper was a marketing message that introduced our new product to the marketplace, and it also used the competitor's logo. The message had been released to our full distribution network the previous day in support of our marketing efforts at the IKECA show.

The problem was that our message was a potential violation of the competitor's trademark and did not properly identify our product. I was mortified. Here I was standing behind the curtain about to address a couple hundred people about leadership and character, and standing in front of me was absolute proof that I was about to become a hypocrite. I did not know what I was going to do. This executive and his team were not happy, clearly, and they had every right to be upset. I told him and his team that I would make it right, but I did not say how, and I could read the skepticism on their faces.

I began my talk by figuratively falling on my sword. I announced to the entire IKECA membership that Omni violated several promises we had made to them and our entire customer base. I told them it was my responsibility to ensure that we operated according to our promises and that we had failed; in doing so, we had printed things about our competitor's products that were untrue. I had tears in my eyes as I accepted this responsibility and promised to rectify the issue with our competitor and anyone affected.

A few people saw my action as self-serving. However, the fact of the matter is that we could have just moved on and said nothing. In the end, the competitor could not and would not have done anything other than to get vocal about the slip our team made. But that was not the point.

I like the people at IKECA, and I like what they stand for. I like our competitors and the people who run them. The competitor is one of Omni's largest customers today, and while they are still our competitor, I teach alongside that company's leader at a KEC training school and co-presented at the 2018 IKECA Technical Conference about the solutions our two companies bring to the market. The influence we at Omni and our competitors have on the KEC market as competent and credible people far outweighs the very slight advantage or disadvantage that may have occurred due to the mistakes we made at that show.

What really drove my fall on the sword was empathy. Our competitor's team believes in their products, and so do a lot of KEC companies. For Omni to duplicate them is a testament to the quality of the solution. For Omni to belittle or defame the quality of the product to such a captive audience in the manner we did is beneath us. I had empathy for us, our competitor and their team, and our customers because we all work hard to bring the best of our work to the industry. To have that work challenged or even displayed negatively in such a public way would be emotionally disturbing; thus, I leaned into that empathetic connection, which allowed me to react quickly and properly in hopes of rectifying the mistake our team had made.

To have empathy for others and yourself shows a tremendous amount of strength. To bear the emotions of others shows an intelligence that not all are endowed with. A common expression for this would be "to walk a mile in someone else's shoes." The ability to do this is astounding to me. We are able to protect, comfort, and even save others with our empathy. My hope for you is that you are an individual with the foundation to have a great amount of empathy or that you are an individual who is willing to try to build that foundation.

Key Takeaways: Empathy

- Empathy is the ability to recognize, categorize, and understand the emotions another person is feeling and then respond in a way that makes the experience comforting, even positive, for all parties. It may also involve feeling the emotions another person is feeling.

- If you want to grow your empathy, consider how your words and actions influence others. Try to see and feel what they see and feel from their perception. Remember, perception is reality, so walking a mile in someone else's shoes will allow you to view the situation from their reality.

- Empathy is not acceptance; it is understanding. Do not confuse the two.

- Empathy can help create an environment for positive influence.

Foundation Reflection

As you reflect on your foundation—where you've come from, the experiences you've had, and those who have influenced you—consider looking at that foundation through different lenses or perceptions. Gaining self-awareness is, in part, learning that we are all developing as humans and that our perceptions have changed throughout our lives. When reflecting on the self, looking through those different lenses, even if they aren't your own and you attempt to view yourself from another's point of view, have empathy for yourself and the positives and negatives of your journey. Consider your current perception and if it is the one you wish to have. Examine every aspect of the true nature of your unique foundation, what makes you *you*, and prepare yourself to have your best influence. Your influence is what makes you an individual.

CHAPTER 6

INDIVIDUALISM

"Very little is needed to make a happy life; it is all within yourself, in your way of thinking."
—Marcus Aurelius

One of the missions of our work is to help people understand that the traditionally accepted definition of "individualism" is no longer valid at this time in history. As we identified in the first part of this book, *individual* to *us* is bigger than a single person; it can be a single individual or a group of people working toward a common goal (capitalized *Individual*).

With that restated, each of us is individual, meaning we are all unique, diverse, and authentic in our own ways. Nobody on Earth is exactly like you. True individualism blossoms under freedom, security, and acceptance. When you take care of and stay true to yourself, you stay individual.

Americans are supposedly the great experiment in individualism. Our freedom can be a dual-edged sword when discussed by opposing minds; it can be seen as unique and positive, but others may label it selfish, egotistical, and self-serving. America, Individually (as a whole country, as one team) is amazing because we are a collection of diverse individuals putting ourselves first (mostly) in an effort to make everyone around us better.

America is way more than a country, though; for many (I)individuals, it is the epitome of hope. There is no other place on Earth where individualism exists for the betterment of all and has shown how that idea can work. Take away individuals' right to speak their minds or choose their own actions, and you take away the spirit of individualism that provides opportunity to every single person who seeks it. Yes, there are exceptions that have uncomfortable, even horrible outcomes. Yes, there are some who exploit the very fabric of what it means to be an individual in an effort to change the definition itself. For example, there are politicians who believe they have the answers to collective problems yet feel they are somehow above those they swore to serve. Likewise, celebrities use their fame and influence to threaten freedom, as it has been defined by the American Constitution. Groups who wish majorities to accept bias and bigotry in an effort to resolve other biases and bigotry are all examples of the dangers *and* joys of freedom.

These aberrations of how I define the true meaning of individualism in America also lead us to generalize our attitudes as individuals—that each of us and our beliefs is more important than another's, which itself fuels the bias and bigotry being created to resolve the generalization in the first place. The reality is that individualism is not selfish. When we slow down and put individual lives into perspective, we understand that for each of us, *I* am *we*. We are the accumulation of all the individuals who have influenced us and, in that understanding, it is clear that individualism is singular, but at the same time, it is so much more, (I)individualism. I think that this realism gets lost on those who focus solely on individual words or actions that are manifested by attitudes (I)individuals can have in the presence of other (I)individuals.

Attitude

Your individualism is an attitude. Your attitude is a way of thinking and believing; it can aid in your perception of the world. Have you ever heard of the phrase "the American attitude?" If you have not traveled a lot or interacted with people from different cultures, you may not be aware that people around the world have identified an "American attitude." That attitude is best defined in the traditional sense of "individualism," indicating that we Americans are arrogant and a bit self-centered. If the American attitude is individualistic, then individualism is a homonym, a word that has more than one meaning. Our attitude defines us and can be the foundation of how people perceive us. Our attitude can affect our position at work, home, and even with friends; in fact, it has affected the very perception of being American at home and around the world. People will go to great lengths to live here. America currently holds the number one spot in immigration.[5] However, the American attitude is just one example of how attitude can present itself in our lives, in both positive and negative ways.

Have you ever recognized someone's energy to be negative and said to them, "What is making you look so upset?" or "What's the matter with you?" These questions stem from our perception of their body language, facial expression, and perhaps even tone; it's even possible that you feel their energy intuitively. If a person has a bad attitude, their body language and tone will show it to the world. We can all experience negative thinking patterns and, thus, create a negative perception of the world and perhaps even of others purely based on our attitude.

Understanding your attitude is part of the self-reflection process, and how we react to situations in our life will be a significant

5. (2022) "World Migration Report 2022" IOM. https://worldmigrationreport .iom.int/wmr-2022-interactive/. Accessed 22 March 2022

part of how we project our attitude to others. Since we can all only control ourselves—our thoughts, words, and actions—we are responsible for the perception we create; in doing so, our reactions become part of our experience and influence each of us, including our attitude. For example, if you are constantly telling yourself that the world is a horrible place because that is your perception, your attitude will reflect that and others will see you as negative. Conversely, if you can acknowledge the positive aspects of the world, your attitude will be uplifted and will reflect your perception. This is often referred to as viewing the glass as "half-full" or "half-empty." Gautama Buddha once said, "The mind is everything. What you think, you become."

Our attitude changes moment by moment, hour by hour, day by day, month by month, or year by year, depending on how we decide to interact with the world and influence our mind. Attitude can even be seasonal; *season,* of course, may be defined in ways that go beyond spring, summer, fall, or winter, as we may have a different attitude during sports seasons. There are even seasons associated with the academic year; if you're a parent, a season could be defined by the period when your kids are in or out of school. I often refer to certain periods of my life as a season; for example, the time we lived in Colorado or Oregon are seasons to me.

If you wish to change your attitude, you must start with transparent and objective self-reflection. How do you talk to yourself in your mind? Are you constantly judging yourself or others? Do you choose a negative or positive way to express what you experience? Can you easily find the silver lining in situations? When you reflect on yourself and your life, you can change your perception by seeing the glass as half-full or looking for the silver lining. Only *you* can manifest the life you want to live, thus changing your attitude toward yourself, others, and life itself. If you look for and focus on the positive in situations, even in those that may seem to be negative on the surface, you can move forward with a mindset that can influence your future positivity. If you choose to focus on the negative in situations, negativity can take over, permeating your mind with negative images, memories, and thoughts. Ultimately, changing your attitude from negative to positive will set you up for success and positive influence.

Key Takeaways: Attitude

- Others can feel our attitude, either through body language, facial expression, tone, or, for some, intuition. This can change minute to minute and influence those around us, either positively or negatively.

- If you want to change your attitude, examine your perception of the world. How you speak to yourself in your mind feeds your perception (the "glass half-full" or "half-empty" can be the difference between positivity and negativity), which, in turn feeds your attitude.

- Gautama Buddha once said, "The mind is everything. What you think, you become."

Maturity

Maturity has little to do with age. Instead, it has to do with interaction, both with self and others, and that interaction creates experiences. Your maturity level is determined by how you interact with the world and how you create shared experiences. Do you respond to others with patience, kindness, and support? Do you work to learn from your mistakes and failures? The perception you create in your mind—your world—will feed your ability to be mature day-to-day. If you continue to grow, evolve, and create positive experiences for yourself and others, or if you attempt to learn from moments where grace is absent, that helps to determine your level of maturity. For example, you can grow in emotional maturity by exercising and drawing on emotional intelligence. Maturity can also pertain to the physical body—being further along in your physical growth through age, exercise, or other health choices.

However, maturity is not synonymous with being a positive influence. An individual's maturity does not denote being on the side of good or bad, just as these opposing forces do not denote an individual's maturity level. To mature means to mature in that which you have created for yourself. If you believe that you can grow and be who you want to be, your maturity level will follow. You create yourself, your perception, and the influence you put out into the world. When you understand that you are in control, only you can decide what your maturity level is. If you mature in, say, being a thief, you may become the best thief there is and attempt more brazen thefts, which ultimately can lead you to punishment for—you guessed it—mature criminals.

Changing our perception requires control. We learn to control things, like our thoughts and reactions, through experience or maturity. Maturity is difficult to define as it is subjective and related to perception, but for our purposes, we will define *maturity* as one who is mindful of and in control of their influence. Our experiences provide the feedback stored in our minds about the causes and effects of our actions. If something gives us positive feelings, we will repeat that action, and we may find a way to do it better, making us feel even better. If we learn how to do something useful, we may use that experience to do it again. For example, if we create a habit of meditating, we may find that it makes us feel centered, present, and in control of our thoughts, and thus we want to keep doing it.

When examining your maturity level, look at different areas of your life to see how you interact with the world in diverse scenarios. The more you can identify about yourself or others, the better. Maturity is part of who we are, but we can work to grow and evolve it just as we can with any other aspect of ourselves.

I have come across some very complex examples of maturity and immaturity. Through my travels, I have been fortunate to meet some young people under the age of 18 who are far more mature than some 50-year-olds I have met. Likewise, the extent of immaturity in some members of the older generations never ceases to amaze me.

One of the most notable examples in my life is a man who, in the eyes of others, has the world by the tail. He is married to an amazing woman whose own professional maturity exemplifies that she has her life together. He is a brilliant business tactician and has a mind that sees things other people miss, from fine details to the most obvious. His ability to develop strategic plans is also impressive. However, his ability to see anything through to completion is severely lacking. He is also amazingly self-centered and sophomoric. His personal maturity level is that of a 16-year-old; people will often see him say or do things in public that you'd expect from a teenager.

The danger of immaturity without correction is that later in life, adults who exhibit such behavior are often dependent on drugs, alcohol, or other vices that lead to premature self-destruction. In fact, I have never met an adult who was socially or professionally immature that did not have at least one vice. In almost every case where I have had to counsel team members or clients, the use of drugs, alcohol, or other vices has been identified as an issue sometime in their life.[6] As peers encounter these types of people and catch on to their lack of maturity and self-control, they tend to avoid interaction with them (consciously or unconsciously) for fear of the repercussions.

Here is one example that sticks out to me when thinking about emotional maturity and how it has played out poorly in the professional world. I was once affiliated with a global company and was on a board of directors that expanded that company's influence. I made the conscious decision to share an email from the CEO of this company, shared with me by his personal secretary, with a friend who struggles with maturity. Upon sharing the email, which

6. (2019) "Link Between Addiction and Emotional Immaturity" UK Rehab. https://www.uk-rehab.com/addiction/link-between-addiction-and-emotional -immaturity/. Accessed 7 March 2022

was sent to me and my fellow board members, as well as a number of very high-ranking C-Suite executives within this company, my friend hit "reply all" when responding to my email with a very sexually derogatory statement. Though I was not the one who made that statement, it had repercussions for me.

We all have a little immaturity in us. My point in sharing the previous example is that understanding maturity and the role it plays in our life is very important. Identifying immature traits in ourselves or in friends or family may be the observation that leads them to change their path in a positive way. However, being on a path to maturity is a habit-building exercise, and creating habits is controlled by willpower.

Key Takeaways: Maturity

- Maturity does not equate with age or being a positive influence. You can be mature in things that hinder you or cause negative influence.

- Know what areas in your life make you feel or act immature. This is part of the self-awareness process and will allow you to be mindful during times when you know you may feel immature.

Willpower

Willpower is like fuel in a vehicle or a charge on your battery; you have to be mindful to refill or recharge your tank periodically. Willpower is the inner drive that motivates us to get through times when we want to quit, rather than do what's needed to reach our goals or final objectives. If we lose our willpower (our tank runs out/battery runs low), we lose that inner support for motivation that can keep us going forward. Once the voice of motivation goes mute, we often find that it was the only thing that kept us going.

For example, for many, dieting is a tremendous challenge. The habits created that lead us to want or need to diet are powerful.

A diet is an agreement with yourself to do something different to affect a change in your health. If you are living an unhealthy lifestyle, it takes willpower to overcome the urge to break that diet (which can run down your willpower battery). Changing your eating habits will be a test of self-control. Cookies, cakes, donuts, pizza—regardless of what tempts you to cheat—your ability to stay true to your diet (and yourself) is led by using your willpower.

As I've said before, multitasking is ineffective and inefficient and will tap into your tank of willpower. Therefore, tackling too many challenges in your life—like creating new, healthy habits in many different areas—is just another form of multitasking. You're draining your willpower when you put effort into breaking or changing habits. Just as you drain your gas tank more quickly the faster you drive, when you put effort into breaking or changing too many habits at once, it drains your willpower more quickly, thus making it more difficult for you to break one, let alone several, bad habits.

As difficult as it is to change eating habits, other habits are just as difficult—if not more difficult—to break. Eating is something that is necessary and should be one of the most basic and simple things we do. Other habits aren't so simple. Smoking cigarettes isn't a necessary function for survival, but it's just as hard to break a smoking habit. The number of habits that take an enormous amount of willpower to overcome is infinite, and our use of willpower doesn't stop at breaking or creating habits.

However, just as your willpower battery can end up at zero, it can also be recharged. Recharging your battery requires you to know yourself and will require different rituals for everyone. This act—charging your battery—is created through self-love and stillness. You may find that reading makes you feel recharged, or perhaps taking a bubble bath does. Going for a hike, walking your dog, watching your favorite movie or TV show, organizing your closet, lighting a candle, drinking tea, playing games, putting together a puzzle, calling a friend, or volunteering (whatever you can think of that gives you energy and wards off burnout) will revitalize you. It is important to recognize when your tank of willpower is running low, as the further your tank is depleted, the longer it will take to refill.

Willpower doesn't just run out due to habit creation. We use it for other human functions, such as working, interacting with others, dealing with conflict, studying, going through hardships, slowing down, self-reflection, and challenging our egos. There is no one way to measure willpower; it is unique to us all. No two tanks are the same size, but it is possible for all of us to expand our tank through exposure, patience, and resilience. Willpower grows with each of us as we grow and mature through experience.

When we lived in Oregon, willpower was a professional struggle for me. By 2005, I had been consulting for 15 years. The role I played at IA changed dramatically when I attempted to slow down my work life and not miss my younger children's childhood as I had missed Kristin's. From 2005 to 2008, my job, for all intents and purposes, was scheduled to be 80 percent focused on the turnaround and development of my client in Oregon. I delegated most of my other work to people in IA I trusted and began to immerse myself in the business of bowling, sports bars, and family entertainment—what a mix!

I enjoyed the less than two-mile drive to work and seeing René, Henry, and Mary every day. At first, I even enjoyed the challenges of influencing change at the company. Change happened very quickly and success followed, which changed my role from consultant to administrator. At the same time, my clients offered me equity in the business, further changing my perspective and responsibilities.

Willpower was the first thing to wane when I became an administrator instead of a consultant. It took all my willpower just to get through a day at work, and there were consequences. During those first three years, I gained a lot of weight and drank more. Using up my willpower just to get through my workday left me with no reserves to maintain the other things in my life that required it: diet and exercise.

As I mentioned earlier, the funny thing about willpower is that it can be regained quickly. Circumstances, choices, and actions can change how willpower works in our lives, and sometimes we don't even notice it.

About the time my first three-year contract was coming up for renewal, we opened our new hotel. As a consultant, back in 2006, before my willpower ran out, my Oregon clients contracted me to conduct a feasibility study about building a hotel adjacent to the family entertainment center. We determined it was feasible. On the day my clients (now partners) decided they wanted to actually build the hotel, they looked at me and said, "Well, since you recommended that we do this as a consultant, now that you're our partner, you're in, right?" And that's how fast I became a hotel owner and manager.

The hotel renewed my role as a consultant for a while. As we built and opened the hotel, the work was once again challenging, and it engaged parts of my mind and experiences that had been dormant since focusing on singular issues for a small number of companies and clients. I learned that it was not the actual challenges that fueled my willpower but the diversity of issues and challenges that kept my willpower full and positive. The funny thing is that, at the same time, I lost weight, worked out again, and slowed down my partying; the willpower to battle those demons was available again.

I have been able to track this roller coaster ride of willpower throughout my life. I know what things in my life take the most willpower. When my life is challenged too much, too fast, and my willpower wanes, the first things to be affected are the things that are easy to give up on. At that point, it's easy for anyone to fall back into a comfortable focus and allow drinking, eating, or smoking to take over.

If you slow down and think about the things that test your patience or challenge your ability to pay attention, you will find that those are the things that use up your willpower. To succeed in the things that challenge you most, you will need to measure and control your willpower. If you can find a way to develop new habits that remove the need for willpower, you have a better chance of reaching your goals and objectives.

Key Takeaways: Willpower

- Our willpower can run out, so it's important to find that which recharges each of us. This could be making a cup of tea or coffee, taking a walk or nap, playing with our companion animal, engaging in a hobby, watching our favorite show, taking a bath or shower, or whatever helps us feel rejuvenated and empowered.

- Just as you drain your gas tank more quickly the faster you drive, multitasking drains your willpower.

- Slow down and think about things that test your patience or challenge your ability to pay attention. These are things that use up your willpower more quickly.

- Sometimes you just need to walk away, take a moment for yourself, and recharge.

Goals

As I sit here contemplating exactly what I want to convey about goals, I realize that almost every self-help author brings this particular issue into their lesson. Setting goals is personal, and we each have our own methods for doing so. However, I do believe that all great goals follow the S.M.A.R.T. process (outlined earlier in this book: S.M.A.R.T. stands for specific, measurable, attainable, realistic, and timely). Without following the S.M.A.R.T. process, you may feel like you don't know how to set or reach your goals. A goal is like a target, but without willpower and being honest with yourself, you will struggle with goal setting and goal achievement.

To hit a target consistently, you need practice. The best way to train yourself to be a goal setter and achiever is to practice goal setting and achievement with things that are easily attainable. I like the analogy of connecting the dots. "Connect the dots" was created to teach children how to draw and follow direction. Learning how to set and achieve goals can be just as simple. You need to establish your goal and make it as realistic and simple as possible. The goal you set is not important here, as this is your practice. Next, think about and outline the steps needed to reach your goal. We will use the weight loss analogy here.

I struggle with being happy with my weight. I carry an average walking weight of about 225; I can get as heavy as 235 and as light as 220. I have been carrying this range of weight since 2010, and before that, I carried it from 2007 to about 2009. In 2009, however, I was able to drop my weight to 205 using a connect-the-dots application of goal setting.

My target weight was 205, and I started at 236. I decided to try to lose 31 pounds in 12 weeks—a short time. I wrote down my goal and looked at the things that affected my ability to stay on target (the things that tapped into my willpower). The biggest issue was consistent weight fluctuations. Due to this issue, one of my "dots" was to weigh in at the same time on the same days each week: Tuesday and Saturday.

My next issue was eating. I needed to track what I was eating to ensure that I could identify the proper foods and nutrition I needed to stay on target. I bought a mini-calendar and logged my food intake there. It was easy for me because I was doing the Atkins diet; today, it's also known as the Keto diet. My "dot" for eating was not eating too many carbs each day, and each dot served as a kind of mini-goal.

By breaking up the ultimate goal of losing 31 pounds into 12 weeks, I was able to track my progress consistently and see the results. This is the measure part of goal setting. When you are losing weight, at times it's very difficult to see that you're actually losing it. As with any goal, if you cannot measure it, you cannot control it, and you must stay in control of your goals. If you make measurement a part of your routine, the goal and "dots" (or objectives) you have set will always be your top priority. The ability to focus on your goal and the smaller tasks needed to reach them is what I equate with being intentional. You must be intentional about your goals; set your intentions, and then act on them.

You can set goals for just about anything and use them to achieve the things in your life you deem important. It does not matter what the goal is—whether it is to lose weight, make more money, or get a job—the important thing is that you slow down, write it down, and then write what is needed to reach it. Everything that is needed to reach your goal is a "dot" on your personal connect-the-dots picture. If a dot requires additional effort to achieve, divide that into smaller attainable actions (dots) that you can reach. If you find that reaching your goal within the original time frame is not feasible, consider adjusting your time frame. All goals can be reached with time.

Goal setting often fails because of unrealistic expectations. After all, you still have an obligation to live your life and take care of your other responsibilities. Adding tasks to your life can be difficult, so give yourself a break and set realistic goals. For some, it may be difficult to complete goals due to the experience of failing to reach that goal in the past. Failure is never a reason to give up on yourself or your goals. If you follow the right steps and have an opportunity to try again, you can turn that failure into a success.

Key Takeaways: Goals

- Remember the S.M.A.R.T. process: Specific, measurable, attainable, realistic, and timely.

- Without willpower and being honest with yourself, you will struggle with goal setting and goal achievement.

- The best way to train yourself to be a goal setter and achiever is to practice with things that are easily achievable.

- Break down large goals into smaller goals, like connect-the-dots, to make progress on your goals more visible. This will motivate and empower you to continue!

Failure

I am always disheartened when I see people give in to the notion that failure is the end. In reality, failure is the beginning. Failure is where opportunity finds us. Success is almost always born out of some sort of failure.

There are an infinite number of examples of people whose failure was the catalyst of amazing outcomes. Henry Ford, Walt Disney, Bill Gates, Michael Jordan, me, and you! Let's begin with some famously successful people who were, at one point, failures.

Henry Ford

"Failure is simply the opportunity to begin again, this time more intelligently."

—Henry Ford

Henry Ford was a failed machinist who had garnered no respect for his work. Ford had a dream and his tenacity and ability to self-reflect and listen to others in the face of almost continuous failure paid off in the form of what is today one of the largest companies in the world: Ford Motor Companies.

Failures can often be rooted in perception issues. Ford overcame a lack of patience for his ideas in a time when there was little to no structure in how shareholders supported businesses. When Ford was first starting off, many were interested in his ideas and eager to see a result. However, Ford was meticulous and spent countless hours reworking designs to ensure they were exactly as he envisioned. This long process turned away many of his potential investors, including some who backed out after giving him money due to their impatience with his process. After his first company was dissolved due to restless shareholders, Ford did not stop working on his revolutionary creations. Instead, he personally listened to the issues holding him back. He had the tenacity to keep moving forward regardless of the challenge or setback.

Despite lacking capital and being seen as too slow to bring his ideas to fruition, Ford reflected on his position and pushed forward. He was grounded in who he was as a person and knew the power of the technology he was trying to bring to the market. He focused his energy on his passion and pursued what he believed to be true to the end. Ford is an amazing example of what it means to be an individual and stay true to your unique influence.

Failure can be used to focus us; it inherently causes us to slow down, take the next step, reflect, plan, be deliberate, and try again. When you choose to keep going in the face of failure, failure becomes a tool to move forward, not an option or excuse to give up.

Walt Disney

"The difference in winning and losing is most often not quitting."
—*Walt Disney*

Walt Disney was once fired for not being creative enough. Today, it's hard to imagine a man like Walt Disney being terminated for his lack of creativity. However, one of his first enterprises, Laugh-O-Gram Studio, went bankrupt—not because of his creativity, but because business can be hard and success and failure often times depends on others. Walt Disney was turned down over 300 times when seeking financing for his ideas. He believed in what his ideas would bring to the market, and his ability to self-reflect, improvise, and stay the course has provided joy for billions of people around the world.

Failure has a way of leading us where we need to go. Failure is not discriminatory in that it is felt at one time or another by every human on Earth. With the right mindset, failure will become a powerful tool in your life. Failure—when seen through maturity or experience and handled with the right attitude—will surely lead to prosperity.

Key Takeaways: Failure

- Failure is the beginning. Failure is where opportunity finds us.

- Failures can often be rooted in perceptions, both those of others and our own.

- Failure is education. It teaches us about what doesn't work so we can start exploring other options for what might become a success.

- Failure is a positive influence. It helps us grow and learn.

Prosperity

In my opinion, prosperity is the positive culmination of all we do. Prosperity is the state in which we feel that all is right in our world, when we are not searching or reaching for something more to make us feel happy. In that regard, it is not always a product of wealth, status, acceptance, or image; prosperity is individual to each of us.

If I were to ask most people, "Do you think *insert name of famous person from tabloid here* is prosperous?" the answer would likely be "yes." However, fame and fortune do not always equal prosperity. Most of what we read in those tabloids is about relationship failure, suicide, drug addiction, and bad behavior. I wouldn't consider any of those things to be true prosperity... would you?

On the flip side, what makes you *content* will make you prosperous. I meet people every day who embrace the life they are given. Many of these people are factory workers, office workers, first responders, and trade workers. Most do not make great sums of money; in fact, many of them struggle financially. They are comfortable with their position in life; though many are working to learn and grow beyond it, some really like the simplicity or regularity of what they do. They are content with who they are, and when you meet them, you can't help but feel their positive energy and peace of mind.

I think of one client in Southern California in particular. His business was a diesel truck repair shop, and he had an amazing location in the Valley, just outside Los Angeles. His shop could handle eight trucks at once and had plenty of space for any size truck. There was also room outside for trucks to park as well as additional workspaces. The company was family-owned and had been in business for more than 35 years.

When I was referred to this client, the business was losing a substantial amount of money. The company had lost direction and struggled to define itself, which should not happen in a *dedicated* diesel repair shop. The shop was disorganized, and the money was day-to-day (the shop needed each day's receipts to create the ability to open the next day). The employees were both disorganized and also day-to-day, meaning that if the receipts were short, the owner might send employees home for fear of not having the ability to pay them. These day-to-day issues created scheduling concerns that further disrupted both revenue and the workforce as jobs were canceled or expedited based on each day's issues. Annual sales were well into seven figures, and, at the time, the owner had reinvested almost a million dollars in losses and capital expenditures, much of it borrowed against the property.

When I first sat down with the owner, it was clear he was unhappy. I was ushered into what I thought was a lavish office for a diesel repair shop. The office was upstairs above the front counter and customer waiting room and overlooked the work area. The owner was dressed in what can only be referred to as "Southern California Preppy." As we began to talk about his business, he kept saying that he wished he could just "turn a wrench" again. He explained his struggles with keeping pace with growth, regulation, changing technology, and money; he also shared stories about employee and customer service issues he faced on a regular basis.

We also talked about his home life. He lived beyond his means, which pushed him to perform better at work or grow the business. He talked about his "friends," who, to me, seemed to be other business owners or professionals who worked in less hands-on positions: white-collar types. After our back and forth, I asked him one question: "What makes you content?"

He answered that less stress and an ability to see his family regularly would make him content, and that he really liked working on trucks. I did not have him elaborate on his family or the stress, as I already knew intuitively what those answers meant, but I did ask him to explain in more depth why he liked working on trucks.

His answer was typical of the people I interview during our BizVision process—the whole experience of working on trucks gave him joy. The challenge of solving the problem is what he enjoyed most at work, and he was good at working on trucks. He liked communicating with truck drivers and other mechanics, both to resolve issues and to communicate the life stories they shared in between truck repair and maintenance. Being on the floor with his team, immersed in his business, was what he was all about; he felt fulfilled from the new experiences each day brought him.

"Why did you ever leave that job?" I asked. He looked at me and said, "I didn't; I just became the boss." Let me be clear: becoming the boss does not imply removing yourself from what you love and turning yourself into a bureaucratic zombie who fits some stereotype created by those who have little to no understanding about what makes companies prosperous.

So, I told my client to take a vacation. He had contracted with us to fix this issue and could trust that in our work with his bank and attorneys, day-to-day issues would be resolved. He took one week off, and we spent the week going about fixing his company. It was a simple one-two punch of decisions; we developed a chief operations officer (COO) position and refurbished the owner's garage area.

The client came back maintaining his status as president of his company. We first showed him his new work area: one of the garage stalls easily seen from his office. Then we presented a work schedule that allotted 60 percent of his time to turning wrenches and introduced him to what a COO position could provide to him. With proper business tools, he could trust what was happening in the office and with his company while he worked with his team shoulder to shoulder.

Today, that company is one of the largest private truck repair facilities in Southern California. The owner still turns a wrench, though now he spends more time with his family, which for him is his prosperity. If you are pursuing contentment, and that contentment is defined by something or someone else, you won't find it. Prosperity is up to *you* to define.

Key Takeaways: Prosperity

- Prosperity is not always a product of wealth, status, acceptance, or image; prosperity is individual to each of us.

- What makes you content will make you prosperous.

- Your prosperity will likely look different than others' prosperity.

individualism Reflection

Your individualism is an attitude as well as an understanding that while you are a single person, you are the culmination of many different influences (people) and experiences. It is also an understanding that you matter and are unique. When you consider who you are, what comes to mind? Is it how you view the world, or perhaps how you respond to it? Is it the goals you set or maybe the way you reach those goals? Do you think those who know you would describe you similarly to how you would describe yourself? To be your best influence, you must first be your best individual;

meaning, you must be the best version of yourself. As you continue to reflect on what makes you an individual human being, keep in mind that every single person is as individual as you. And in our individuality, we can all be influenced to change from an *I* to a *we*.

CHAPTER 7

BIAS

Written by Mary

> "The eye sees only
> what the mind
> is prepared
> to comprehend."
> —Robertson Davies

We typically accept our bias—our judgments—as if they are objective thoughts because they are so deeply ingrained within us. Normalized societal inequalities—based on appearance, accent, socio-economic status, education, gender, ethnic heritage, and so much more—are part of the root of our bias. Our biased thoughts are powerful, and they may negatively influence ourselves and other people; these thoughts are often tied to and confirmed by our life experience through what is referred to as confirmation bias, which means that we look for the world to represent what we already "know" to be "true," rather than looking for signs that disprove our own beliefs. Confirmation bias further solidifies all our biases. This means that we are conditioned and programmed by our external influences to accept things as true and as an extension of our own influence—so much so that we don't even realize it has become part of our way of thinking. Confirmation bias is so powerful and successful because the mind wants to protect itself against being challenged, leading to further and more deeply ingrained bias.

Now, I want to make a clear note here at the beginning that bias is not synonymous with racism. Racism is an active and conscious acknowledgment, while we are typically unaware of both our unconscious and subconscious biases. (More about the differences between unconscious and subconscious bias later.)

In the following sections, we will attempt to understand the difference between unconscious and subconscious biases and how they affect us all. True self-reflection must be done with eyes wide open and as much objectivity as we can give ourselves. On your journey to find your most positive influence, unearthing your biases will be an important aspect of being your most positive self because often your bias can influence your thoughts and actions, sometimes unknowingly, and cause your influence to actually be negative instead of positive. Understanding bias in yourself will allow you to help others understand their bias in whatever influential circumstance you find yourself.

Unconscious vs. Subconscious Bias

It seems there are at least two problems standing in the way of having a larger discussion about bias, including unconscious and subconscious bias. As a team, we identified the potential largest inhibitors of discussions around unconscious and subconscious bias to be: 1) varying definitions of the unconscious and subconscious mind, and 2) the fact that people are lazy and want an easier out for their bias; they claim their biases are unconscious to avoid the guilt and accountability that typically comes with confronting bias.

Subconscious bias is not yet regularly discussed among psychology experts; however, we will attempt to spark that discussion to provide you further insight into your foundation as an individual. First, we want to spend a moment unpacking these potential inhibitors.

It is difficult to have a concrete discussion without universally accepted definitions of unconscious and subconscious bias. For the purposes of this book, we rely on definitions of the unconscious and subconscious minds taken from psychology. In psychology, there are three parts of the mind: conscious, subconscious, and unconscious.

To start, the conscious mind is probably the most familiar to you. The conscious is your current awareness, thoughts, and actions. When you think about what you know—your memories, daydreams, and even emotions—those predominantly lie in your conscious mind, which is easily accessible. Information that lies within the conscious mind is easy to recognize and discuss with others or ourselves rationally.

In opposition to the conscious mind is the unconscious mind. The unconscious is inaccessible, a place where our mind represses and keeps memories and information from reaching our conscious and even subconscious minds. Your unconscious mind is not a place you can simply access on command. Conversely, the subconscious is far more accessible to our conscious mind, usually appearing to us in the form of dreams, snap judgments, reactions, and bias; it also controls our reactions and automatic responses. For example, if you make a snap judgment about someone, you may begin asking yourself some questions as to why it occurred. If you are able to easily uncover a memory or belief that led to your judgment, then that bias is most likely rooted in your subconscious, where it is more accessible. However, if you fail to identify where this judgment came from, it could be inaccessible to you and rooted in your unconscious.

When you can identify where your feelings of bias stem from, they typically reside in the subconscious. When you can't identify your bias, it's most likely unconscious. We are of the opinion that the differences between these kinds of biases aren't being discussed due to intellectual laziness, lack of exposure to diverse ideas, a wish to keep things simple, or a desire to remove accountability from the conscious self. It's easy to dismiss negative feelings of blame and guilt if we can pin our biases on being located in our unconscious. A compounding issue here is that we are unsure if these reasons are due to unconscious or subconscious thinking. Regardless, we want to attempt to spark a conversation around these different types of bias so that we can better understand each other and ourselves.

To reiterate, unconscious bias is bias that we cannot explain or identify. When it presents itself, we don't recognize it as bias, we don't know where it came from, and we accept it as the truth. Unconscious bias is something we remain completely unaware of. Unconscious bias cannot be discovered on your own; it is impossible because it is a true blind spot in your way of thinking. This means that unconscious bias is reflected in thoughts we don't question, because why would we?

Then, there is subconscious bias, which stems from our life experiences, including our upbringing. Subconscious bias doesn't remain hidden from us for long, especially if we begin the process of self-reflection. Subconscious bias can even come with compassion and empathy for the self as we explore the reasons for our bias and understand our own experiences.

Regardless of whether your bias stems from your unconscious or subconscious, it's important to keep the following information in mind. Bias is a natural part of the brain; it's part of your evolutionary programming that was originally meant to keep you safe, and because these systems are so primitive, we typically don't even realize when they occur. Our biases can make us feel attached to our idea of self, leading us to feel that we are owed something or we've been cheated out of our right to something. It takes an extraordinary amount of effort to combat our unconscious way of thinking.

So much can go on inside the mind that we aren't at all or fully aware of, and these unconscious and subconscious ideas shape our influence. Just as we can easily become lost in comfortable focus while driving, our mind will autopilot our bias regardless of whether it stems from our unconscious or subconscious mind. However, unlike comfortable focus, being in the present moment won't help us identify our unconscious bias. We likely do not easily identify subconscious bias in the present moment; it often takes self-reflection on our experiences, thoughts, and actions to understand and come to terms with our bias.

What is terrifying *and* fascinating about bias is that it is as much a part of us as our conscious thinking and beliefs. Typically, learning that we have these unconscious or subconscious processes, and trying to be more aware of them, is how we can combat their effects. To recap, our unconscious bias is that which is unknown to us; even upon self-reflection, we are not able to discover our unconscious bias as these are foundational thoughts stemming from culture and nature. Subconscious bias is more accessible, but only if we wish to become aware of it. Subconscious biases are shaped by the experiences we have in life and nurture. To combat and become aware of any bias, it takes time, courage, patience, acceptance, accountability, and humility. In doing so, you will prepare yourself to be more mindful of your influence on others and how you interact with your teams.

Key Takeaways: Unconscious vs. Subconscious Bias

- Bias is a natural part of the brain; it's part of our evolutionary programming that was intended to keep us safe.

- In psychology, there are three parts of the mind: conscious, subconscious, and unconscious.

  - **Conscious**: The conscious is composed of your current awareness, thoughts, and actions. When you think about what you know—your memories, daydreams, and even emotions—those predominantly lie in your conscious mind, which is very accessible. Information that lies within the conscious mind is easy to recognize and discuss with others or ourselves rationally.

○ **Subconscious**: The subconscious typically controls our reactions and automatic responses, and when we are able to identify where our feelings of bias stem from, it is subconscious. Identifying subconscious bias takes self-reflection on experience, thoughts, and actions in order to understand and come to terms with it.

○ **Unconscious:** The unconscious is inaccessible, a place where our mind represses and keeps memories and information from reaching our conscious and even subconscious minds. We cannot explain unconscious bias and we are unaware of it. We don't recognize it as bias, we don't know where it came from, and we accept it as the truth. Unconscious bias cannot be discovered on your own; it is based on instincts that we don't naturally question.

The Identification Process

Identifying our own unconscious bias is impossible without the help of outside influences. Unconscious bias is so hidden that it may go unnoticed our entire life or until someone else has the courage to point it out. On the other hand, we can identify our subconscious bias upon self-reflection, or it may be pointed out by outside influences. This is a pivotal point in a relationship, and it's a scary one.

Just because someone challenges you to confront what they identify as bias doesn't necessarily mean that it is, in fact, bias. You will need to consider their point of view, your values, and where the thought came from (if it's subconscious) and why before deciding if it is truly bias. When your bias is pointed out, regardless of whether it's subconscious or unconscious, your mind often works to protect itself by attempting to protect the status quo. When your ways of thinking are challenged, it produces a myriad of results ranging from aggression and guilt to outright denial. Our minds produce these results because we generally don't like having our worldview challenged. We evolved to protect ourselves and our tribe, and in doing so, we have developed tendencies that make us inclined to be biased against that which opposes us. We actively seek information that confirms what we already believe to be true, and we deny anything that doesn't fit what we already know or believe. Our minds deny information, even the truth, to make us feel better and, in turn, not confront being wrong.

Part of the reason we do this is because we become mentally or even physically uncomfortable when we have our perception challenged. To protect us from discomfort, our mind rushes to a place of denial and dissociation or distraction where we know our beliefs are validated, giving us emotional, mental, and even physical security. Therefore, uncovering and uprooting bias is an active decision, and one that must be made to enhance your positive influence. We must give ourselves permission to grow and learn, telling ourselves that we can, in fact, change our minds about things. Only we have the power to control and challenge our own minds.

The more we understand our conscious, subconscious, or unconscious behavior, the more influence we will have over our learning and growth. When we gain a better understanding of ourselves and society, humanity will be better as well because society as a whole falls back into sub- and unconscious action. However, with the boom of technology and the ways it connects the world through the internet, we have the power to change how the *world* works and how we all think. But it all starts with us challenging ourselves, giving ourselves permission, challenging others, and choosing to be a positive influence.

Even once you have made the decision to be open to learning, growing, and evolving from your unconscious and subconscious bias, uncovering these biases can still be difficult. How do you find something that you don't consciously recognize or realize is influencing you? This is where humility becomes necessary because, unfortunately, you typically can't uncover your bias alone. When it comes to your subconscious biases, you may be able to uncover them if you are honest with yourself and take the time to reflect on your experience. Regardless, think of biases as blind spots. The most efficient way to uncover your bias may be to ask others to point it out to you and, when they do, to accept that it is a positive action that will help you grow. This will require immense trust, care, and respect between you and the other party.

However, one day you may find that someone points out a bias that takes you totally by surprise. I'll digress to the first time my generational bias was pointed out to me by my professor. It was truly ironic that learning about my bias came about in a class where we were learning about unconscious bias. I'm currently working toward my master's in organizational leadership. My program is online, and each week we have a different module to learn the concepts. In one of my weekly submissions, I made a comment that I believe the world is changing and becoming more open-minded because younger generations are connected through and raised with technology. My professor was quick to point out that it's not just younger generations that are becoming more open-minded because of technology, and she correctly pointed out that I have an age/generational bias.

At first, I denied it. I thought, *She doesn't understand what I'm saying. She's not seeing my point. I don't have a generational bias.* However, once something is pointed out to me, I can't let it go. So, my train of thought didn't end there. It took me a few days of thinking about it, but I concluded that she was onto something I had not realized about myself. Something as innocent as a belief in open-mindedness among younger generations uncovered a mountain of bias. It's biased to think that just because younger generations were raised with technology and in an environment that values social awareness that they are more compassionate, giving, and fair.

It's rooted in an "us versus them" mentality, which is something inherent in many of us.

For me, my individual world lens is a little like this: I was born into a world that appears to be on the brink of collapse, battling social injustice and climate change, to name a couple of ills. This has been hard for me because I deeply cherish diversity, authenticity, social awareness, and care, and I feel a strong connection to our Mother Earth. My primary driver in life is benefitting society—helping individuals and Individuals—by minimizing suffering in one way or another. My secondary driver is protecting the Earth. These feelings are at the very center of my being—my highest values. I have proved my commitment by being vegan for almost seven years, which is not a sacrifice I made for myself. It's the path that makes me feel like I am doing the most to uphold my values with the choices I make every day. I protect humanity and the Earth by choosing to be vegan. From my perspective, our Earth was handed to us by past generations; ones that, to me, seem to care very little for humanity and our Earth, or we wouldn't be where we are now. This is where my generational bias is rooted, in my subconscious mind, but that doesn't make it right or fair.

My experience with learning about my bias is exactly what research shows. My mind went to outright denial, and this was coming from someone I respected and trusted: my professor. It shows how hard the mind works to protect itself, but why? One reason is that it's easier to do things the way we have always done them, which allows us to stay comfortable; another reason is that even the most loving and righteous people have bias, and it's hard learning you do. Often, our biases go against our conscious values and beliefs; that's how pervasive and hidden they are. I fully believe in accepting individuals for their authentic selves, and, in doing so, I believe we must respect that they are unique in many ways. I also value diversity, so being told that I had a bias against entire generations was shocking because I would never consciously think that way. Generations share similarities based on the time and lens they grew up in, and just because I have experience with some closed-minded Gen X and Baby Boomers doesn't mean that all people in those generations are closed-minded. In fact, I currently have some people in my life that are proving that people from older generations do, in fact, act in compassionate and open-minded ways.

I was able to overcome the denial of my bias because I have a constant thirst for growth—a growth mindset. I have to constantly remind myself that I have the power to change my mind and perspective and that I don't have to be a slave to my mind's natural processes. Reminding myself of the power to change is a habit I have accepted and continue to work on. This constant reassurance in my ability to grow and learn is why I didn't let that comment go. It's why I take criticism positively and objectively, not lightly. I am always looking for ways to improve and have a more positive influence on myself and others.

Reactions to Bias

Through this process, you need to give yourself permission to grow and learn, but you must also have empathy for yourself when you learn about your bias or any negative character or personality traits you discover (because we all have them). You are not alone, and you're not a negative influence just because you have a bias. In fact, the opposite is true. Being open to learning and challenging your bias makes you a positive influence because it takes courage.

Just by hearing another person's perspective and giving yourself permission to challenge your current way of thinking, you become a positive influence for yourself and others. You help yourself to be a better influence in the future, and you show others that it's okay to be wrong, to have bias, and to question yourself so that you can more deeply align with your conscious beliefs and values. It will be difficult to come to terms with the fact that bias lurks within all of us, but change is a process, and even the most positive change can be a challenge.

You will first need to work on identifying the immediate negative response you have when your worldview is challenged. Do you have more of an emotional or a physical response? Do you feel anxious, angry, guilty, or afraid? Do you experience chest tightness, butterflies, or even headaches? Getting to know how you respond to being challenged will help you overcome those negative responses in order to get more comfortable being questioned and growing from that process. Once you understand your immediate response, you can commit to resolving that response in a positive way.

It's important to note that if we share unconscious bias with others, those biases will be blind spots to both the other person *and* us. This is why we need diverse outside accountability to help us recognize what some may not identify. Third-party support is the path to positive change. We need to rely on people to assist us in becoming more consistent in our ways of thinking, staying true to our values, and continuing to grow in our positive influence. This will only happen if we are willing to listen to others' opinions. While it is a difficult task to entrust to others, without third-party support, it would be nearly, if not completely, impossible to recognize our own biases.

The next time someone correctly points out my bias as my professor did, it won't be so daunting because now I have experience with it and have prepared myself for the process of understanding and addressing my bias. It seems easier to face something after you already have experience with it. At the time, I felt irritated and guilty for being accused of having subconscious generational bias, but I came to terms with the fact that we are all human, and that means we all have biases.

We need to show patience for others and ourselves while we confront bias and push humanity to level up in our understanding and actions of influence. I do still believe the boom of technology has accelerated this "level up," but I am more open to seeing the possibilities with all of humanity, rather than just younger generations.

Another key point I would like to make when uncovering our bias is that we are still valued. Something that often occurs when discussing or discovering bias is a feeling that we are no longer valued, which stems from our defensive response against being asked to acknowledge a blind spot. As stated previously, this response can stem from feelings of guilt because our biases can often go against what we value or believe. You may be lucky and not experience any negative emotional or physical consequences when challenging yourself to uproot your bias. However, research shows that you will, most likely, experience some kind of negative symptom as your mind works to protect the status quo. These feelings can range between sadness, anxiety, stress, guilt, anger, disappointment, regret, shame, shock, denial, and more. Your experience is your own, but it's important to keep in mind that most individuals have some kind of negative response. This will help you identify your negative response, if you have one, so that you are able to lessen the effects over time. Once you gain more experience challenging yourself, the negative consequences of doing so should lessen.

One reason these negative symptoms occur is that our values and beliefs are very personal to each of us. Therefore, learning that our own mind hides beliefs from us that go against our consciously committed values can be shocking and devastating for some. It can make us question ourselves and the reality we have created. It's a scary feeling to question our worldview, and we may worry about the idea of being a hypocrite. However, learning about our bias doesn't make us hypocrites; it doesn't make us any less than we are, it doesn't mean we aren't valued, and it doesn't mean we have a negative influence. In fact, it means quite the opposite, should we choose to challenge ourselves and become aware of our bias. We all have biases that need to be tackled, so don't feel alone. Feel empowered to be someone who challenges your way of thinking and enter leveled-up humanity. Here, you are creating a more positive influence for yourself and those around you.

It can be difficult to know how to respond in the heat of learning about your bias. We need to employ empathy and patience for both sides of this equation. As someone pointing out a bias, have empathy for the other person's common response of immediate rejection for protection. The easiest way to have empathy for those who respond negatively to their bias being uprooted is by educating yourself like you are now. When you understand where both unconscious and subconscious bias come from and what may happen to someone when they learn about it, you open yourself up to empathy for their situation. Understand that pointing out bias could include a negative response. Therefore, remain calm and compassionate, and, if the other party is willing, try to engage them in questions that will allow them to come to their own conclusion about their bias. To do this, you will also need to listen to how they respond. What is the emotion they are feeling? Where might that emotion stem from? Employ excellent listening skills, coupled with your empathy, to keep the conversation as positive as you can.

If you are on the other side, as someone having their unconscious bias pointed out, have some empathy for the person pointing it out because speaking up is intimidating. It takes courage to be honest and speak from a worldview that identifies bias. While it may be difficult to have empathy for them if you immediately have an unfavorable response to their observation, it's important to try to remain compassionate and engage that person in conversation. Engage in active listening to understand what the other person is saying and ask follow-up questions to get a better idea of their worldview and why they think this is a bias. Don't negate their opinion just because you don't agree immediately. There may be some truth in what they are saying, and you owe it to your personal growth to consider their worldview. If you don't challenge yourself to be better and do better, you won't ever grow into your highest potential.

Often, challenging bias produces negative emotions on *both sides*. That is why being open, empathetic, and listening in order to learn is the best thing you can do. If you have offended someone, do not immediately deny their feelings to save your own. While you might not agree with where they are coming from, offending and hurting someone's feelings should never be your goal. Apologizing and putting yourself into someone else's shoes (and worldview) could open your mind to learning much about life. You may walk away learning nothing, maybe even disagreeing. However, when you strive to have a positive influence, you strive to follow a path that hurts the least amount of people and helps the most. Listening to others and being present in order to learn from them and how they view who you are from *their* worldview can only bring positivity. The more information you have, the better.

One big reason humans shy away from this topic and their own personal growth is that we like to take the easy way out of things. We don't naturally enjoy putting work into something because working means depleting our energy more quickly. Our minds are hardwired to conserve energy for ourselves, especially if we are already pessimistic or in a fixed mindset (which do not always go hand-in-hand; not all those who are pessimistic are fixed-minded and vice versa). Putting effort into learning about ourselves and who we are takes energy and time, two commodities that seem to escape us in our fast-paced world of immediate gratification. This whole book is about learning about *you*, uncovering your foundation to stand in your highest power, and having a positive influence. You are doing a disservice to yourself if you do not spend your life getting to know who you are fully. And if you don't, then nobody will. We fully believe that you deserve to be known. You owe it to yourself to understand yourself as a unique individual. Commit to fully understanding yourself, even your blind spots.

Key Takeaways: The Identification Process

- We all have unconscious and subconscious bias, so don't feel alone. Feel empowered to be someone who challenges your way of thinking.

- Identifying your subconscious bias can be done upon self-reflection, or these biases may be pointed out by outside influences.

- Unconscious bias is so hidden that it may go unnoticed until someone else has the courage to point it out to you. Rely on this support.

- Only you have the power to control and challenge your mind; show yourself compassion and empathy and give yourself permission to grow.

- Once you understand how you respond to learning about your bias, commit to resolving it in a positive way (if you agree with the one who pointed it out).

- Have empathy for those who respond negatively to their bias being pointed out, just as you should have empathy for yourself.

Types of Bias

There are some main types of bias to be on the lookout for. Understanding these may even help you identify some areas you may want to work on or address. One we mentioned previously is confirmation bias; this type is present when you refuse to draw conclusions based on reality and instead draw conclusions based on personal preference, beliefs, values, and desires. One way to combat confirmation bias is to ask yourself if you're being truthful or missing any information that could be pertinent; you may even enlist outside accountability to identify if you are missing any facts.

Another common type of bias is affinity bias, or similarity bias. When we are under the influence of this kind of bias, we easily connect with others who look like us or have similar interests, backgrounds, experiences, or personalities. This can cause assimilation, which, mentioned previously, is when everyone conforms to present themselves in a similar fashion to the leader or culture of the group. It can also cause issues of discrimination against groups you are not part of, meaning if you have affinity bias, you could reject different genders, ethnicities, and more. While this isn't inherently negative, it can become negative if we begin to take action and reject those who oppose us. A tool we can use to combat affinity bias is to hold compassion for those who are different or even in complete opposition to us. While we may feel most comfortable around those who think, look, and talk like us, that doesn't mean we need to be averse to the other. Keep in mind that without your opposite, you cannot define yourself. A coin needs two sides to exist, so have gratitude for that which is your opposite.

A few other common biases include height, weight, and ability bias. These all fall under a beauty bias, which is the belief that the more attractive people are, the more qualified, competent, and successful they are. By extension, we believe that those who are taller, thinner, or able-bodied are more qualified, competent, and successful than those who are shorter, larger-bodied, or disabled. While our minds may trick us into thinking the way someone looks defines their level of competence, this is simply not true. What matters is someone's mind and heart, not how they look. Challenge yourself to overcome these beauty biases by looking deeper, past what you can see. What skills, talents, education, or personality does this person possess? How do they treat others and themself? Consider the adage, "Don't judge a book by its cover." How many times in your life have you wrongly judged someone at first and later found that you were wrong?

Next, there are biases that lead us to put people on a pedestal or condemn them for eternity. This is known as either the halo or horns effect. When we learn something impressive about someone, we tend to place them on a pedestal and begin to ignore their shortcomings in favor of one or a few remarkable facts we know about them. Conversely, if we learn something unpleasant or negative about another person, we may condemn them forever, ignoring even their most noble characteristics. One of the best ways to get over this bias is to come to terms with the fact that we are all human; we all make mistakes, and we all have positive and negative qualities.

Another type of bias that can sometimes, but not necessarily, combine the halo and horns effect is contrast bias; this type of bias is when you compare two or more things, leading to an exaggeration, either positive or negative, of one or more of those things. This one is difficult to break from because it's one we all do almost daily. Comparing and contrasting is how we make a lot of our decisions. To avoid this type of bias, determine if you have any standards for what you are comparing and start there. If there are no standards, fall back on your personal values. You may even ask yourself if you are exaggerating any of the claims you are making or if you are being wholly truthful with yourself. Perhaps you may decide to enlist aid from trusted outside accountability.

Additionally, there are biases that many of us are familiar with: gender and age bias. Gender bias is the tendency to prefer or recognize one gender as superior to another. It is the idea that women should be nurses, caretakers, kind, compassionate, and obedient; conversely, gender bias is the idea that men should be doctors, sole providers, hard, emotionless, and dominant. These ideas damage all genders, as emotions, intelligence, and characteristics are fluid rather than binary. Then, there is the ageism bias, which is the tendency to believe that age equals competence. There is sometimes a misconception that ageism is only a bias if you reach a certain, older age; however, ageism can happen at any age. While an age bias may lead you to believe that someone who is older may be less competent, the same can be said about someone who is younger; it just depends on your bias. Regardless, individuals should be judged and measured based on merit and what is inside, not based on appearance, gender, or age.

In the workplace, you will see all kinds of bias play out each day once you know what to look for. Along with those mentioned, other types of bias in the workplace are performance, likeability, attribution, and maternal bias. Performance bias is the assumption that some groups are more capable of succeeding in their tasks than other groups. Unfortunately, once performance bias starts, it morphs into a belief that the more dominant group (the group that is perceived to be more successful in completing tasks) can be judged on their potential for the future, while the less dominant group will be judged on their accomplishments rather than potential. This places a heavy burden on the less dominant group to perform.

Likeability bias tends to coincide with gender bias the most in the workplace; this bias stems from societal beliefs that men should be assertive while women should be kind. Therefore, when either men or women break from this norm, meaning if men behave kindly and women assert themselves, if we have a likeability bias, we will like those people less. Attribution bias is when we make assumptions about others' behavior that lead to inaccurate conclusions about that person. This is similar to the halo and horns effect.

Finally, in a surprise to no one, there is a severe maternal bias in the workplace. Maternal bias is the assumption that just because women become parents that they are no longer committed or willing to commit to tasks and projects at work. While this can be a blanket parental bias, it doesn't affect fathers in the workplace as much as it affects mothers. However, it will affect fathers who want to be more engaged with their children, often leaving the rest of the team wondering why that individual is "uncommitted" to their work when, in reality, they value family and wish to be a good parent. Should fathers be discriminated against in this way, it would be similar to a likeability bias.

There are lots of biases to be on the lookout for, and we are about to make it just a little more complicated. Have you heard of intersectionality? Intersectionality is when an individual belongs to more than one minority group, which can compound discrimination against that individual based on the groups they belong to. Some examples of intersectional identities are an Asian transwoman; a white, disabled, gay man; a Black lesbian with children, or an overweight, elderly Indian man. However, intersectionality and bias are not limited to race and gender; individuals experience compounded discrimination based on their sexual orientation, gender identity, ability, appearance, religion, mental capabilities, and so much more.

When considering your biases, you must keep in mind the individuals who are disproportionately affected by bias for simply existing within multiple minority groups. You can become an advocate for the fair and just treatment of all people within your organization if you have the courage to speak up. If you're hoping to overcome all bias in your life, you must expand your mind. Remain curious about the world and about others, rather than choosing to be judgmental.

Key Takeaways: Types of Bias

- **Confirmation bias** is when we refuse to draw conclusions based on reality and instead draw conclusions based on personal preference, beliefs, values, and desires.

- **Affinity bias or similarity bias** is easily connecting with others who look like us, have similar interests, backgrounds, experiences, personalities, and more.

- **Beauty biases** such as height, weight, and ability bias are the belief that the more attractive people are, the more qualified, competent, and successful they are.

- **Halo or horns effect** biases put people on a pedestal or condemn them for eternity. When we learn something impressive about someone, we tend to place them on a pedestal and begin to ignore their shortcomings in favor of one or a few remarkable facts we know about them. Conversely, if we learn something unpleasant or negative about another person, we may condemn them for life, ignoring even their most noble characteristics.

- **Contrast bias** is a combination of the halo and horns effect when we compare two or more things, leading to an exaggeration, either positively or negatively, of one or more of those things.

- **Gender bias** is the tendency to prefer or recognize one gender as superior to another.

- **Age bias** is the tendency to believe that age equals competence; ageism can happen at any age.

- **Performance bias** is the assumption that some groups are more capable of succeeding in their tasks than other groups.

- **Likeability bias** tends to affect gender the most in the workplace; this bias stems from societal beliefs that men should be assertive while women should be kind, for example. Therefore, when either men or women break from this norm, meaning if men behave kindly and women assert themselves, if we have a likeability bias, we will like those people less.

- **Attribution bias** is when we identify a flaw in another individual and then attribute that flaw to their success and failures; this means we will give that individual less credit for their successes and more blame for their failures.

- **Maternal bias** is the assumption that just because women become parents that they are no longer committed or willing to commit to tasks and projects at work.

- **Intersectionality** is when an individual belongs to more than one minority group, which can compound discrimination against that individual based on the groups they belong to.

Unintended Consequences

When and if bias is not addressed, there can be unintended consequences. These consequences typically present themselves after bias has influenced an act, decision, or word choice, or they are born from our inability to point out another individual's bias, making it that much more important to point out bias in others. One example of the unintended consequences that stem from not addressing bias is holding people back in the office through discrimination.

Holding people back at work can mean several different things, including negatively influencing the recruiting and hiring process, and who to promote, recommend, or mentor. These types of discrimination are typically done unintentionally, but they play out in organizations across the globe. Consider how many women or how many people of color are managers, C-suite employees, or sit on boards of directors compared to the demographics of that company's lowest level. Even the most diverse companies struggle to bring diversity up the ranks and keep each level as diverse as the last. Why is this? It's rooted in unaddressed bias.

When we allow unconscious bias to influence our decisions, like when recruiting, hiring, promoting, or mentoring, we may be ignoring a better candidate with more potential. The processes by which an individual joins an organization and moves up the ranks should be based solely on merit, not what they look like, their gender, sexual orientation, parental status, or any other category in which we are all diverse. This is where affinity bias comes into play, as we tend to gravitate toward those who remind us of ourselves. It's our ego's way of bolstering our own self-confidence and making us feel more important, valued, safe, and like we belong. Affinity bias is completely normal and nothing to feel ashamed about. Again, we are hardwired to behave this way. What's important is that we begin to recognize these pitfalls and try to overcome them. Denying that these pitfalls exist will only perpetuate the behavior.

When looking at recruiting, hiring, promoting, and mentoring, ask yourself if those candidates were chosen for their merit. Were there other candidates who would better fit the position? Why weren't they chosen? By looking back and examining past decisions, you may be able to uncover your own or your team's most prominent bias types.

Another frequent and unintended consequence of bias is alienation or making others feel like they don't belong. When we don't understand our bias, it's possible we can offend and alienate others without even knowing. This most frequently happens when others don't feel confident or safe enough to speak up, thus internalizing their feelings of alienation. While we may not intend to alienate or exclude, it does happen often. A seemingly harmless comment can make others feel negatively about themselves, influencing them to cease being their most authentic self in that space. When people feel alienated or like they don't belong, it can lead to a myriad of issues for a team. If you have ever experienced alienation or felt like you didn't belong to a group, you know what it feels like and may recognize some of these characteristics: absenteeism, decreased creativity, decreased productivity, low or no emotional engagement, increased stress-related illnesses, and increased accidents caused by not focusing or slowing down. Avoid alienating others by creating a culture of belonging; this starts with you being open to growing and uncovering your bias.

Helping a diverse set of individuals feel like they belong takes time, practice, and patience. It takes the want to grow, be open-minded, and learn from missteps. Some of these missteps may be rooted in unconscious bias; for example, if you say the wrong thing and offend someone, it probably wasn't your intent, but it does become a good learning experience for you not to repeat that same mistake. Let the other person know you are open to learning and growing by understanding how you offended them, from their perspective. Remember that perception is reality, so to be a great leader and be the best version of yourself; you must let go of your ego and meet others where they are to better understand them. This increases your cultural intelligence and helps team members feel like they belong. Nobody is perfect, and some days we all feel alienated from the group. What is important is that we rectify those feelings of unimportance and ensure that those around us understand their value, regardless of the mistakes they make. Growing into the type of leader who promotes diversity and inclusion takes patience and humbling of oneself, but it must be done to foster a positive culture.

Finally, a third and prominent unintended consequence of bias is overgeneralization. While many biases are rooted in over-generalization, we tend to, as a society, overgeneralize unconscious bias itself. This is part of why we have attempted to tackle the difference between unconscious and subconscious bias in this book. By overgeneralizing the type of bias, it can cause confusion, low accountability, and avoidance. Additionally, it can lead people to believe they are above this phenomenon, tricking themselves into believing they are special and immune to the human condition of bias. This is their ego telling them what they want to hear so they can remain comfortably in the dark regarding their blind spots. The mind does this to protect itself against having to change, grow, and be more aware of the world.

Do not trick yourself into thinking you are special and above bias. You aren't. We are all human, which means we all have bias. There are no dividing lines when it comes to the mind's inner workings. We know it can be scary and uncomfortable to try to change your mind and grow. However, it is necessary if you want to make a positive difference in the world.

Key Takeaways: Unintended Consequences

- Recruiting, hiring, promoting, and mentoring individuals should be based solely on merit, not what they look like, their gender, sexual orientation, parental status, or any other category in which we are all diverse.

- A frequent and unintended consequence of bias is alienation or making others feel like they don't belong.

- Alienation can cause increased absenteeism, decreased creativity, decreased productivity, low or no emotional engagement, increased stress-related illnesses, and increased accidents caused by not focusing or slowing down.

- Helping a diverse set of individuals feel like they belong takes time, practice, and patience.

- An unintended consequence of bias is overgeneralization, which can cause confusion, low accountability, and avoidance, leading people to believe they are above the human condition of bias.

- Unconscious and subconscious bias are rooted in all our minds, and they are part of the human condition.

Bias Reflection

Overall, unconscious and subconscious biases are rooted in all of our minds and they must be examined with patience and compassion for ourselves. We must not feel negatively toward having bias, as it is a natural part of the human condition. However, we have evolved to the point of control that allows us to examine and understand ourselves in ways that humanity has not been able to before. We have access to the world through technology and the sharing of knowledge, so we have the perfect platform to work on ourselves and grow. It may feel nerve-wracking for some of us to search and identify bias in ourselves, but it is necessary for our future. Only you have the power to control your influence, which means only you have the power to control your mind. While you may not be able to control every facet, such as bias, you can control how you respond. Commit to your personal growth and move with us toward leveled-up humanity.

CHAPTER 8
COMMUNICATION

How we communicate matters. From the words we say, to the words we write, to the inflection or tone of our voice and our body language, communication is powerful. In fact, communication is the key to success in almost all situations, as most personal conflict is the result of a lack of or misunderstanding in communication.

Some of the most revered people on Earth were able to gain so many supporters because of their impeccable ability to communicate. People will follow someone into great glory or great misery because of that leader's singular ability to instill courage and conviction through their words. Whole societies are influenced by leaders' charismatic communication, which can either divide them or bring them together. Furthermore, when communication is consistent and repeated by many, regardless of whether what is being communicated is true, individuals or whole societies can perceive that communication as reality, which may even alter history forever.

When I think of that last statement, I am reminded of some of the people we celebrate and despise when we look back on history. Through his own oratory and the propaganda of his regime, Adolf Hitler encouraged an entire nation (and people from multiple other nations) to get behind the fascist movement and all that it stands for. His influence on society had individuals doing and accepting atrocities that are clearly recognized as abhorrent today. Right alongside Hitler were people like Josef Stalin and Mao Zedong, who promoted communism through coercive communication, also known as propaganda.

On the positive side of history are individuals such as Abraham Lincoln, whose eloquence and inspiring messages about freedom led to the abolition of slavery. In the 20th century, Martin Luther King, Jr. carried on in that spirit to spearhead a civil rights movement for African Americans. Think about what motivational speakers like Tony Robbins have done for countless people through his influence and teachings. It goes to show that people follow those who communicate well. Men died under George Patton's command because they believed in what the general communicated. Patton instilled bravery and alleviated fear to the point where men ran into certain death to preserve freedom for people an ocean away.

Being a great communicator takes more than the ability to just say words. It takes a passion for conveying what you believe is right or wrong. That passion can be transferred to others, both through words *and* action.

For me, communication is a skill I must work on every day. I am not a great orator, and I do not think of myself as a great writer. However, I like to speak and love to write. Since 1990, I have relied on either René or Mary to edit my public writing so that I convey what I truly intend to say to my audience. Through the years, I have certainly improved my skills; their edits have decreased, and my own words have become more thoughtful. I wrote my first book before meeting René back in the late 1980s, when I met Jack Danger (whom I have previously mentioned as a major influence on who I am today). One of the things Jack taught me was how to prepay a mortgage. He instructed me on how to use the amortization schedule to pay off a mortgage early and how to calculate the return on investment (ROI).

I applied that basic knowledge, coupled with some ignorance and even less writing ability, to create a booklet explaining this program in a structured way. I then came up with the idea to hold seminars in restaurants where, for $75, individuals could come get a meal and learn how to apply the teachings in my booklet to their personal mortgages. Unfortunately, it was an amazing failure.

I think that maybe 12 people showed up at a restaurant called the Wagon Yard in Northern Phoenix, Arizona, 3 of whom were my uncle, father, and stepmother. I had printed a few hundred books, but after that disappointing beginning, I set that project aside for more fruitful work like installing computerized accounting systems.

Fast-forward to 1990, when I met René. She edited the original booklet, and through the randomness of life, I met a guy who was also in the prepaid mortgage business. I resurrected this literary work of art and once again set out to sell the program. This time, I sold it for $29.95 in bulk via mail order ads in magazines and newspapers. I even convinced someone to go out and sell this program to people door-to-door. I think I sold another 12 (maybe a few more than 12, but not many more).

In the end, I sold the entire program to a company that did mortgage acceleration work; they took it and made it marketable. The lesson for me, however, was that communication is powerful. I'm not sure I thought this consciously at the time, but at some point, I realized that my original writing brought value to people. My style of writing was the catalyst for someone else to take what I started and turn it into something marketable. My ability to identify an issue and communicate solutions had value.

Foundations of Communication

Communication built our first company. Improving my communication also expanded my insights into other opportunities. The overall scope of our entire organization is built on the foundation of communication. We begin all projects by learning about our clients and how they communicate, and it is from this original understanding that we help our clients affect change in order to reach their goals. My journey to learn the full value of communication was not complete until 1994, but it was in 1991 that I began to learn the value of *self*-communication (which is discussed in the next section).

During the early years, my deeper understanding of organizational continuity began to affect my work. From 1991 to 1994, we identified the deficiencies in our clients' companies and then developed a systemized solution. We carried about this work when PC-based accounting systems were just beginning to be widely adopted, and it was a struggle to convey the advantages of these systems at first. This period marked the beginning of the transition from written and spoken word to electronic communications.

One of my early ERP (or in layman's terms, accounting systems) implementations was for a company that managed documents and sold document management equipment. This company had a robust digital records conversion business where it scanned documents onto either microfiche or what, at the time, was new: saving to a hard drive. This company's early migration projects from paper to digital platforms gave me an early look at the future of communication. Back then, there was a sense that the world could and would go paperless, but, as we have learned, this has yet to completely happen. However, what we have done is change how quickly and efficiently every (I)individual can communicate to the masses.

During this time, I was learning about how local area networks were becoming more robust and allowing better collaborative communications within the smallest of businesses. We had to develop a way to quickly introduce these advantages to potential users, and our method involved designing and using lessons. To accomplish this in a new world of technology, we used flow charts and message mapping to present information in both a visual and written format, which was new to most small business people at the time. To build my skillset in this area, I read a lot of books about presentations and writing, but I also found that writing and speaking are very different. When we write, it is much harder to convey our true emotions and passions than when we speak. Emotion and passion may be easy to convey for a romance, murder mystery, or horror story, but expressing passion or emotion in more objectively driven business issues like accounting systems or computer networks is amazingly difficult.

From 1991 to 1995, we still did most of our communicating via written and verbal exchanges, and the written word was delivered via paper. We became proficient in writing these outlines and still use the same format today.

In 1995, AOL became a prominent player in business communications. The ability to deliver written information instantly changed our approach to communication; however, we did not yet know how dramatic this change would be. Our ability to influence the market became less costly, and the access we had to our target audience opened up. However, we also began to see a rapid acceleration of human communication that created challenges, like going too fast.

The internet and the access to communication tools it offered also gave us a new way to help our clients communicate. Leaders could immediately deliver messages to individuals or an entire organization with a single click. Teams could update managers on progress as it happened, without having to speak to anyone. Documents could be shared electronically, in real-time, from desktop to desktop.

The entire dynamics of how we communicated was turned on its head. As email took off, technology continued to improve. Today, we can send a note to anyone on the planet from our phones and it can be read almost instantly. We can send documents, conduct research, and influence change in seconds.

Self-Communication

Looking in the mirror is what I call self-communication because it is one way we talk to ourselves in our minds: We use those moments to understand how we analyze ourselves and others, the stories we tell ourselves about our experiences, and how we shape our perception. However, self-communication entails being transparent with yourself, just like a mirror transparently shows you what you look like. The first step to being honest in life is being honest with yourself. Although I am sometimes guilty of being dishonest with myself, it never ceases to amaze me the number of people who do so without a second thought.

Imagine trying to design a product while your partner constantly lies to you about the budget. Would you be able to trust anything your partner said? Imagine all the time lost developing this product because of ineffective communication. If lying cannot serve as the basis for effective communication in a team setting, then it certainly cannot work for self-communication.

When considering how to begin communicating with yourself, I recommend starting with writing (either physically in a journal or digitally). When you write to others, they may not understand your tone and emotion; however, when reviewing your writing, you will know the emotion that fueled it. You will be intimately familiar with the context behind the words you write and read. Writing things out provides us the opportunity to release the emotions that build up in our lives in a healthy way—privately, if we wish, and at a slowed-down pace. Try to view your journal entries from a third-party perspective, act as though you are another person reading your entries to help you find and highlight flaws.

When you begin to communicate more honestly with yourself, you will notice that you communicate with others more clearly. One of the biggest challenges when communicating with others is that they do not have the benefit of knowing your internal thought process. This missing context means they do not always know where you are coming from when communicating, or what you hope to achieve.

For example, sometimes I already know how certain aspects of a particular recommendation will affect my target audience before I make the recommendation. Unfortunately, this means that I may begin discussing the benefits before I've laid the foundation, and anyone who does not have the proper context is unprepared to hear my communication. Since my audience does not necessarily know what I know or have the same perception, context matters.

Context is a part of communication that, when misused, can alter your future. I was recently involved in an ERP project where a manager did not want to take responsibility for his actions. To skirt responsibility, he took pieces of emails and strung them together to create a narrative that removed his responsibility from the situation and diverted the focus to others. The high-level manager would do this often, both in writing and in person. This is how salespeople and journalists—professions that are typically celebrated for above-average communication skills—can really cause havoc in the world.

When you miscommunicate issues and leave out context, the decisions made going forward will be flawed. For example, in the instance with the ERP system, some underlying contractual obligations were not conveyed in detail. The managers took parts of the contract and used only those specific parts to communicate with their team, giving their team a false understanding of the contract terms and leading them to believe that the terms were changeable. The terms of the contract, however, were not able to be altered. The contract had specific terms, and those terms negated a number of solutions that were being considered by the team.

These issues are rooted in self-communication. At some point, the people offering partial information had to consider the truth as they used context to disrupt the programs in place that were contributing to the company's more viable future. I cannot count the number of projects that I have been asked to join that went bad due to individuals taking facts out of context and attempting to make them work to their advantage, not to their customers' or constituents' advantage. Sometimes this is unintentional; sometimes it is not. The originators could almost always resolve or avoid the unintentional issues if they had reviewed the issues with a more objective mindset.

Self-communication must be truthful to benefit you. If you find yourself in the company of those who like to twist words and construct a misleading narrative, you will find that keeping documentation of events will help you tremendously. You can do this by saving emails or by writing down the discussions you have with said person and sending your understanding of the conversation to them in an email. If you do this, be sure to ask them to reply with any additional information or if you are understanding the conversation from similar perspectives. Doing so will document these conversations and give you written word as proof should they try to be hypocritical in the future.

Key Takeaways: Self-Communication

- Proactively recognize the lies you tell yourself to enhance your self-communication skills.

- Remain honest about your actions and reactions, as this is key to understanding yourself.

- Writing provides a healthy opportunity to release the emotions that build up in your life.

- When challenged by people who lack context or clarity in their communication, follow up with your understanding and include context and points of clarity for verification.

Self-Deception

One of the most dangerous actions we take when we deceive ourselves is justification or, better stated, self-justification. When we use self-justification to excuse behavior, we are lying to ourselves in a way. We see this occur almost daily in our life. For example, each time a person does not take accountability for something and then justifies their action, they are self-communicating this deception, as well as communicating it to anyone influenced by their actions and justifications. We often do things in life that we know are destructive, and we tell ourselves that doing so is okay if it does not affect others, or we justify it by telling ourselves the effect is not "bad." But what is the effect on you? Shouldn't you protect yourself from any destructive behavior?

The impact of deception (and self-deception) is common in work environments. We once had a team member who often complained about their workload. They repeatedly asserted that they did not get the help they needed from the team, going so far to share that they felt other team members falsely touted a positive team environment that they, in fact, felt was not positive for them.

This same person announced on a Tuesday that they would be gone the following Thursday and Friday. Upon returning the Monday following the leave, this employee said that no one did any work to support them in their absence, thus proving a lack of teamwork.

I spoke with this team member after they complained about the situation, and I asked them to identify the differences between them and their team members. I specifically wanted to know why they were a good team member and why their peers were not. They provided the example that they always cleaned the office, always said "yes" to any task requested, and always did their best to accommodate a peer's request.

I then asked them these two questions: "What did you do before announcing your departure on Tuesday that would have set up your peers to support you? And what cost has there been when you say 'yes' to everyone's request, regardless of the fact that, in your words, your workload is already too much?"

At this moment, the team member seemed to get it; they, too, were contributing to the discourse and chaos that they were pawning off on others. I ended my discussion with this person by saying, "In the end, my partner and I are ultimately responsible for the chaos you and your peers are experiencing." I was going to go on to say something else, but this employee cut me off and aggressively nodded; they stated, "Yep, that's right. It is all your fault—you set us up to fail." Sometimes, people need to justify everything and may never be able to understand how they have contributed to an issue. Human nature may be to deflect responsibility for things that create a perception of negativity. One of our biggest challenges is to accept our actions and work to move past them in the most positive way possible for everyone influenced by them.

I was in a board meeting recently where I heard a board member justify violating a noncompete clause. They said that, within the confines of the board meeting, the violation was justified because the actions of the company whose clause we were violating justified our actions. The company whose clause we might be violating was also violating their own contractual obligations, and this was the member's justification. At the time, there was an open discussion about using information from the team member who caused us to violate the noncompete clause. The board member who had justified the violation led the discussion. It did not take long for one of the other members to challenge the board about this violation; the silence after that admonishment was palpable.

This is highly destructive behavior. When challenged, the member who violated the noncompete finally admitted that the justification was a cover for not doing what was right in his mind; showing that two wrongs don't make a right. The fact that one board member would confront the other is a good example of going beyond self-communication; if you're in a meeting and telling yourself that what you are hearing or reading is wrong or untrue, but you continue to allow it to go unchallenged, you become part of that communication failure. If you challenge the miscommunication, you offer the possibility to turn the failure into a success.

The consequences for this violation were nonexistent for the organization but quite high for the member who justified it. There have been a number of conversations between peers on the board that questioned the integrity of the members who justified a contractual violation. These questions may hurt the integrity of the overall board, as an undercurrent of distrust now exists among the members.

Our actions have consequences, regardless of our own impressions. All actions have a reaction. Life is like a pinball game of action and reaction, constantly bouncing through time. Being honest about our actions and reactions is the key to understanding ourselves as individuals. This honesty comes from within and expands outward to our sphere of influence.

Being honest with yourself is generally hindered by fear. For some, it can be scary to look within and truly get to know yourself, but with self-communication, you can let go of that fear. Who should know you better than you know yourself? We often fear that honesty will hurt, be hard to deal with, or elicit a negative reaction from an outside source. Once we go beyond that emotion of fear, we just might realize the overall effect that a lack of honesty will have on us and our community.

One way to tackle self-deception is to write or journal your challenges. Each time I feel challenged to be honest or need help making a decision, I write the issues down and then read about them as if I am a third party. I have found that reviewing my decision-making process as if I were an outsider has helped me to better understand it. However, what this process has revealed scared the hell out of me.

I have noticed in my journaling process how irrational I can be with certain decisions and/or choices. As I continued to develop my ability to communicate with myself regarding my thoughts and actions honestly, I noticed that my decisions became more thoughtful and that my propensity to fool myself was reduced. However, regarding very individual or personal decisions (with a high emotional or financial impact), I can still fool myself. You, too, will find that there are times in life when self-deception will take over, and you need to remain mindful.

Key Takeaways: Self-Deception

- Do not let fear hinder your ability to be honest with yourself.

- One of the best ways to tackle self-deception is to write or journal your challenges and read them back to yourself as if you are an objective third party.

- Our actions have consequences, regardless of who we think our actions influence. All actions have a reaction.

Written Word

In 1992, I found myself working with a company that audited utility bills for large companies. My former company, Business Accounting Solutions (BAS), was contracted to install computers and software and manage the implementation of systems to manage document workflow more efficiently. I was then offered an opportunity to invest in this client's company. This opportunity would prove to be prophetic, as it laid the foundation for our current business structure.

This company was very successful at the time. I was a couple of years into building my business in Denver, and the opportunities for me, my family, and our company were tremendous. However, we ran into problems early, as do many private partnerships with many investors. I was 26 and eager. I borrowed money from my mother-in-law to fulfill my financial needs for the contract and investment.

As a result of my youthful zeal and ignorance, I found myself the president of the company at a time when the company found itself in the middle of legal action with independent contractors and vendors. My new status as president trapped me in the middle. I was in way over my head; I found myself in meetings with shareholders I had never met and never even knew were involved in the company. My days consisted of nonstop phone calls and back-to-back meetings.

Becoming president was a case of being in the wrong place at the right time. I had been calling the offices of this company every day to get paid; the company owed BAS about $240,000 and owed the other vendors about the same. BAS had supplied most of the equipment, software, and installation. As a new shareholder, I was getting a little upset, having just borrowed $15,000 from my mother-in-law. I wanted this to be a good, first, private external investment for us.

For about a week, I called twice a day trying to reach the then-president or vice president. A receptionist answered with the company name. Finally, I got tired of calling and getting no calls back. I drove to the office, which was on the 10th floor of a 12-story building in Aurora, Colorado. When I got to the office, it was locked. At the time, I had a cellphone, but reception was spotty, so I walked down the hall and asked if I could use the phone. I called the company, and to my surprise, the receptionist answered. When I told her that the doors were locked, she explained she was an answering service in downtown Denver.

Things moved quickly after that. The building manager agreed to open the door because, as we found out later, he had not heard from the tenant, and the rent had not been paid. When we opened the door, the office was empty: nothing.

The founders who originally brought me into the organization all disappeared, along with the majority of the assets we sold to them. The missing assets had a value of over half a million dollars, including computer systems and software provided to the auditors and a full document management system that scanned documents and put them on CD-ROM—a huge step forward in early 1990s technology. To put it mildly, I was freaking out, standing in that office like a deer in the headlights.

One of our vendors had a relationship with an excellent law firm. The vendor's wife was an associate at the firm and introduced me to the senior partner. When I sat with him for my first meeting and recounted the past six weeks of business with this company, he gave me one piece of advice that stuck: Always follow up a conversation that can affect you with a written note. Determining which conversations can affect you is amazingly personal, especially with decisions that have legal or financial implications. Others may include policy, procedure, or any topic where a third party may be influenced. The senior partner in this law firm explained that the note should review the conversation and ask for immediate clarification if anything in the written note is inconsistent.

He then went on to explain the value of this practice. He had been through a nasty divorce recently. He had adopted the act of sending a written note whenever he had a conversation that included agreements, promises, or decisions by either party. During one conversation with his ex-wife, they had agreed to an amicable split of a certain debt. His attorney followed up that conversation with a letter to his ex-wife and one to the lender that detailed the conversation and agreement. Neither the lender nor his ex-wife responded to his letter.

Later, during the final divorce proceedings, his ex-wife and the lender both wanted him to pay the full debt. He told them that he and his soon-to-be ex-wife had agreed to different terms, and both his ex-wife and the lender challenged him for proof, to which he responded by providing a copy of both letters he had sent to them as a review of the original discussion. The judge ruled that he did not have to pay the debt in full.

In the end, the written word helped us to resolve the situation above, where I became the president of a company in a very precarious position. We got control of the company with the corporate documents we had; the original shareholders and officers were all gone. We involved the local police, who at first were less than helpful, saying it was a civil issue over which they had no jurisdiction. We managed to salvage a few of the contracts the independent contractors had signed, but that only prolonged the death of the company. The company eventually ceased to operate, leaving me with almost a quarter-million dollars of debt.

The end to this story is both good and bad. The documents and agreements we were able to salvage through public filings and legal actions finally showed that none of the remaining shareholders were involved. I worked out a payment agreement with the original equipment vendors. Almost two years later, I received a call from the FBI. The original vice president had been found dead in Ohio, and in the same town, they found cash and computers in a storage bin; those assets were distributed to the victims of the theft. I learned that the written word had influence. The written word has more power than the spoken word in cases like this because it has legal permanence.

In my case, writing is foundational to my productivity and organization. It provides me the support I need to take action. It creates the trigger I need to spur me into action and complete the task I agreed to finish. With writing, I have the foundation to remember tasks much more easily (as I have previously discussed during accountability). There is a rule at IA: Never just tell Brian something; send it to him in written format so he won't forget. Writing makes information concrete and creates a sense of urgency. The written word, when used properly, can also bring a sense of closure. Why else do we put signature to paper when agreeing to 30-year mortgages or lifetime marriages? Our written signature binds us (I)individually to the words on the page.

Key Takeaways: Written Word

- Always follow up an important conversation with a written note. The note should review the conversation and ask for immediate clarification if anything in your written note is inconsistent with the conversation.

- Sometimes the written word has more power than the spoken word because it has traceable history and legal permanence.

Communication Reflection

Honesty is always the best policy, so strive to be honest in all you do. This is particularly important when communicating with yourself. If you aren't honest with yourself first, you can't be honest with others. Many find honest self-communication difficult due to fear of knowing oneself, upsetting others, or addressing failure. However, to be your best influence, you must know yourself fully. This knowing starts with honest self-communication. On your journey, continue to reflect on how you deceive yourself or create justifications to make yourself feel free of accountability. These areas need your attention. If you need to take a pause to write, do so. There are times when the written word can save you, help you see clearly, and reflect on the truth.

CHAPTER 9

USING INDIVIDUALISM FOR INDIVIDUALISM— THE ULTIMATE OXYMORON

> "Individual commitment to a group effort—that is what makes a team work, a company work, a society work, a civilization work."
> —Vince Lombardi

Being great for yourself first so you can be great for others may appear selfish to some who don't understand your positive intention. Those who view this focus on the self in a negative way may find that putting yourself first (even if it's for the betterment of others) is a selfish drive to take resources you may not need. While there are dangers in teaching people to put themselves first, our hope is that you will do so for the right reasons. The danger comes from those who put themselves first out of ego instead of a drive to give back and be themselves. They might then take advantage of others or exaggerate the concept of individualism and try to benefit at the expense of others; therein lies the key differentiation.

In order to be the best for others, you must have the best to work with. Defining what is best for you is amazingly subjective, so only you can know what this means. However, if your effort to be the best and have the best support possible comes at the expense of others, then that which you defined as the best cannot possibly be the best—at least not in the context of (I)individualism as we see it. Better put, our best self is best for us and for all those (I)individuals we influence so they, too, can be their best selves.

First, as I touched on already, what I define as "the best" is not the same as "the best" for someone else. Our experiences, expectations, and perceptions of life alter our definition of many things, including what we attribute to be "the best." When people's realities are different, they need different things to succeed. For example, someone who experiences anxiety will need different tools to achieve success as opposed to someone who doesn't experience anxiety. When you think of being the best, it needs to be in the context of your own ability.

Think about how someone might say they are the best plumber in town. What does this actually mean? Are they "the best" because they have more experience in plumbing? Is it because they have more employees? Is it because they charge the lowest prices? As mentioned, "the best" is subjective to each individual's experience, expectation, and perception.

Defining what "the best" is for you is an important challenge that I hope you will tackle. When you define your best and can achieve that, you will better understand what it means to influence others in your most positive way. While it is possible to be a positive influence at all stages of your life, the more aligned you are with your best self, the easier it is to consistently influence others in a positive manner. Therefore, finding your best means finding what your individual advantages are.

Our technology company, System Design Consultants (SDC), was founded in 1997. Our IT salesman was the driving force behind our going from start-up to over two million dollars in annual revenue.

He was one of the best we had the pleasure of employing. He had a knack for connecting with people, and he took the time to understand what he was selling. While he worked for us, he sold IT services.

One day, he walked into the office and said he wanted to be our vice president of sales; he laid out what he thought that position would look like. Now, at this time, we had about five or six consultants, plus myself and one administrative person. We were a small company. This individual wanted a six-figure salary, a car, and other perks that are often seen in large corporations. He also wanted an office and expense report.

To put his personality into context, I'll give you a little backstory. When he was hired, René and I decided to invite him over to our house for dinner. This house was our first Thornton home and was built in the 1970s. We remodeled it ourselves, so it was a modest 1,887-square-foot triplex. René and I owed about $70,000 on the house, so our mortgage was very small compared to those of our peers. When he and his wife arrived at our home, we talked about the company and our goals. Then he looked around our home with his wife and said, "Well, those are great plans because it's obvious you're no Rockefeller."

He then proceeded to counter propose me on a multi-level marketing program he did on the side. He was very persuasive and obviously fixated on the material things he would gain by reaching his personal goals. I wanted anyone that persuasive, dedicated to reaching goals, and fixated on making money on my team. He spoke as if he would go to almost any professional lengths to afford pretentious stuff, and he also possessed the ability to speak eloquently, making him a great asset to our new IT company.

Back to his demand to be VP of sales. We told him "no" on the title of VP but offered another fancy-sounding title. We explained the value of the position and how influential it would be for him and our company. Furthermore, we shared that his success thus far had likely stemmed from his natural sales ability, and that we needed him to sell. We were not in a position to hire another person in an administrative role, which was what he really wanted.

On his 358th day of work, 7 days shy of his 1-year anniversary, he walked in and quit. He informed us that he had been hired as the VP of sales for a new start-up IT company in Boulder. He went on to tell us that with this position, he would get a $60,000 salary, commissions, and a new Lexus. For context, his base with us was $24,000 a year plus a nice commission. He had made no less than $15,000 a month for the past 5 months. He was also sitting on project work that would make him even more money in the next year. However, since he had not worked for the company for a full year, he was not yet vested.

Five weeks later, he returned to the office and asked for his commissions. We paid his final check in full for all he earned up to his 358th day. We explained that he quit his job 7 days ahead of his vesting, so he forfeited $35,000 in commissions. Boy, was he pissed. So much so, in fact, that he publicly called our senior administrator a "fat fucker" before he left.

Over the next few weeks, we were targeted with threats and more derogatory comments, and then all went quiet. On a Monday, about six weeks later, he walked in asking me for his job back on the terms we originally gave him. I said, "no."

This individual was an amazing salesman. However, when he used his individual power to be a part of our Individual company, it proved to be toxic. I did give him advice on how to develop himself to better work with a company like ours. IA was in its infancy, but I had already started developing the philosophies that are here in this book. My advice to him was this:

> You need to go out and focus on being the best you that you can be so that those you influence can benefit. You cannot expect to be accepted for what you have done in the past or what you will be and offer in the future. Your value in the present is that you have a natural ability to develop and keep relationships

with clients. Flexing your ego is hindering your ability to work in an Individual (team) setting. The company who offered you what you wanted failed by not providing the individual advantages needed to succeed. So, go out and refine your sales skills and learn what it means to be a leader. Come back when you think you can work as part of a team and not just for your own gain.

He did just that, and during the time he was gone, we merged our company with a much larger one. He ended up coming back about 18 months later and integrated into our team nicely. The combined revenue of the company grew to over $7 million, and we had a top-notch sales leader. He stayed on for a couple years, worked with the team, and later became a successful VP of sales.

The lesson here is to hold yourself and those you influence accountable. Doing so will allow you to forgive others, give them a second chance, and continue growing in your positive influence. If this individual had not grown during our time apart, he wouldn't have been able to rejoin our team and help us achieve Individual success. Additionally, if we had not been accountable to our policies and procedures (with regard to his failure to become vested), we would have set a new standard for all employees. We all must remain accountable, regardless of relationship status. Even though I liked this man personally, I wouldn't have been able to welcome him back to our team if he had not taken it upon himself to grow in his positive influence. If you fail to hold yourself and others accountable, you may end up putting the cart before the horse, and the horse may get away from you.

Accountability

One of the things we taught our children early on was that we should be held accountable for our actions. These actions include speaking as well as doing. In our home, we are accountable for the things we do. However, being held accountable is not the same as having negative consequences. This point is often misinterpreted when I am speaking to people. Just because you accept accountability for something does not necessarily mean there will be a negative consequence.

We believe there are two types of accountability: self and outsourced. Self-accountability is when we hold ourselves accountable for our thoughts, words, and actions by being honest with ourselves. Outsourced accountability is when someone else holds us accountable for our words and actions. Accepting personal accountability or being accountable for what we say and do through outsourced accountability is part of our maturity level. Growing up, I was not taught accountability *at all*. There was no understanding of the word or what it might mean to me. My actions through childhood demonstrated this fact, and I did almost anything I wanted... until I got stepparents.

Two months before the end of seventh grade, I moved to California, where I got my first lesson in accountability. I was in chaos emotionally, and my parents had just divorced for the second time. I was angry from the constant moving, and I acted out a lot, but no one paid attention, so my anger went unchecked; this amounted to building a foundation of non-accountability.

When I arrived in California, my family was living in a condo close to the school I would attend, called Los Cerritos. This school looked like a prison compared to the ones I had attended in Illinois, and I was about to enter into it without knowing anyone. My entire education up until this point was in private Lutheran schools with class sizes of around 20 students. My classes in California at this public school could be more than twice that size.

In my first week, the bullying began—just like in Illinois. By then, I had reached puberty, so I now had physical size and my pent-up anger to use to my advantage and fight back (react). In that first week, I got into a fight, had three days of in-school suspension, and had to meet with the counselors. They talked to me about managing my stress and how acting out meant that I would be held accountable (outsourced accountability). At the time, the concept of consequences or accountability did not register because I had no foundation to support or reconcile the statements made by these people.

However, this introduction to consequences and accountability fell on deaf ears because my mind was not in control, and they had never followed through on anything like this before. Like learning all new habits, accountability must be implemented regularly and consistently. I was in new territory, so I did what many humans do when confronted with accountability: I acted out. It got to the point where I was so miserable in California that I made a stink with my parents, and to the chagrin of my stepparents, I was granted permission to move back to Illinois. Bill, my stepfather, thought it would be better if I adjusted and adapted instead of bouncing between homes when I was uncomfortable. In hindsight, he was probably right.

Unfortunately, my move back to Illinois put me right back into chaos. My father married Michele, who was 21, and I was 13. I was not allowed to go back to Immanuel Lutheran, so I went to Dundee Middle School. Up to this point, Michele paid about as much attention to me as my father did—she was not only young, but she was also pregnant. We lived in an apartment, my 9th home in 13 years, which we shared with her father and brother.

I adapted better to public middle school in Illinois. However, after the first week of school, a teacher took me aside. His questions about my home life were really jarring, so I just told him we lived in Village Quarter with my dad, my stepmother, her father, and her brother. He then asked me if anyone had ever talked to me about hygiene—essentially, he was asking if anyone was providing outsourced accountability for me at home.

I told him "no" because I still did not understand what he meant. He proceeded to tell me that I smelled and needed to take a shower. He explained to me that I was not taking good care of myself, and because I was entering puberty, I needed to take hygiene seriously and hold myself accountable. This was the first time I had heard of holding *myself* accountable. He was not mean about it; he was just concerned.

Conversations like these can be acutely embarrassing, but as I look back at this moment years later, I realize that this was my first lesson in self-accountability. At the time of this difficult conversation with my teacher, I was finally beginning to understand what it meant to be accountable for myself and to myself. I learned that I needed to be accountable for my actions and for my body; if not, there could be consequences such as being further marginalized by the other kids. My teacher often asked me if I was doing better with taking care of myself. He mentioned on a number of occasions that he recognized I was showering and doing well; he also called me out if I came to school with oily hair or body odor. He even bought me deodorant once. He provided me with more outsourced accountability than I had up until that point in my life.

After my brother was born, things quickly changed because my stepmother discovered that being a mother gives you control and influence in a different way. In eighth grade, I had a few rules applied to me by my parents, but having a curfew was a new one. Before the birth of my brother, no one held me accountable for where I was, and nobody cared if I was late. After he was born, Michele became much stricter and began to hold me accountable for my actions. One of the consequences she levied against me for being late was that I would be grounded one day for each minute I was late. She implemented this because I was always late, and, due to the lack of accountability, I was flaunting the freedom as only a teen can do. In what seemed like the blink of an eye, we went from no accountability to this—without a middle ground, I bet you can imagine how an immature teen would view this action—and from a young stepparent to boot.

In a matter of six weeks, I learned two lessons about accountability that were dramatically different … but I was learning. Through the rest of my school years, almost all of my accountability came from third parties as outsourced accountability: teachers, other parents (friends and step), bosses, friends, and the police.

I lasted through ninth grade with my stepmother and father. Ironically, Michele began to really try to be more of a mother figure to me during my freshman year of high school. She began to pay attention to what I was doing, offered some help, and even gave me my own bedroom so that I would feel more comfortable at home. A week later, however, I informed them that I was moving back to California.

My stepfather was a bit more involved, but he had a different way of parenting. For one thing, I had assigned chores, and if I did not finish them, he grounded me. In my mind now, this was in line with what being accountable as a teen *should* be. However, there were some odd lessons mixed in. For example, Bill had access to movies before they came out. We often would watch a movie on VHS weeks before it was out in movie theaters. In this case, Bill's actions were teaching me that if you could find a way not to get caught doing something that was not right, you could avoid being held accountable.

The inconsistencies of my early life lessons paved the way for me to push the boundaries as a junior and senior in high school and I learned how to justify my actions to myself. Accountability became a game that, when played by adolescent teens, could quickly turn dangerous. Illegal drugs and guns, and the violence that accompanies them, were unfamiliar to me while growing up in Illinois. California was a place that would expand my relationship with all of it. This toxic mix taught me more about accountability in the next two years of my life than in all my years beforehand.

My introduction to drugs was not as a user but as a supplier. I was offered an opportunity to sell drugs to kids at my school, more specifically, at parties on the weekends. Over the next 15 months, my actions reinforced my complete lack of understanding of accountability and consequences. As I began to use drugs in my senior year, my life changed, yet again. People held me accountable for the things I was doing, like not completing homework and ditching school. This would eventually culminate in me being given a choice to either go to jail or go into the military (the ultimate place to learn about accountability).

The circumstances that led to this lesson were pretty simple: I was out of control. One night, I went out to deal drugs and because I also did drugs, I left a bunch of them in my mom's car. My mother found them and decided to turn the drugs into the police. They were not my drugs; they belonged to the person who supplied me. The supplier took matters into his own hands and burglarized our home while my parents were out of town as retaliation. In an effort to resolve this in a way that avoided consequences and account-ability, I tried to make a deal with the dealer. During that process, when I arrived home to settle up with my parents, they had turned the issue over to the police.

I was taken to jail, booked, and then taken to county jail in Ventura, California. On day two, I was visited by the police again; this time, they expanded my charges. When I was arrested, I also had a gun in our home that my parents gave to the police. It had been stolen from Oklahoma long before I ever had it, and apparently, it had been used to commit crimes. Even though I had never been to Oklahoma or had anything to do with the gun being stolen or used, I was now facing charges that included possession of stolen material and possession of a stolen firearm that crossed state lines.

On day five in jail, my girlfriend's family put their house up for my bail, and I bonded out. I was given a public defender, and my parents essentially disowned me. During the negotiation pro-cess I learned of my choice: military or jail. The military option ensured that the charges would be expunged at some point in the future and would not follow me, so I chose the military and com-munity service instead of going to jail. I did not really understand the impact this accountability would have on me; at the time, it seemed the most unaccountable choice, a simple slap on the hand. However, when I actually performed community service and entered the military, my choice and the level of accountability became quite clear and made me reflect more on my choices. The military is tough and wearing an orange jumpsuit while picking up trash is embarrassing.

Now, accountability and consequences are something I consciously consider with my actions. We all can use help holding ourselves and others accountable. If we go through life and allow ourselves and others to escape accountability, then we instill habits that can prove to be amazingly destructive to our future.

For example, if we are not held accountable for being late, we may miss opportunities or be labeled as unreliable. If we are not held accountable for our promises, we may be labeled as untrustworthy. If we don't hold our children accountable, they may mature into adults who won't be accountable or teach accountability to those they influence.

Being accountable is not negative. If we agree to something, then we should expect to be held accountable. If accepting the consequences is more tolerable than fulfilling the action you are being held accountable for, then you will still be held accountable for the choice to accept those consequences. When I know that I cannot hold myself accountable for something, I solicit family, friends, and employees for help with outsourced accountability. While there are always exceptions, I do all I can to make sure that I hold myself accountable so that I am consistent in following through with my obligations.

If you are consistent in holding those you influence accountable, you can reinforce that accountability is a positive thing. This, in turn, can produce people who will be more self-accountable. Being consistent in all things is the optimum way to gain the results you want. When I am journaling my solutions to issues, I will often look back on other decisions to ensure consistency. I know that if I am inconsistent, there may be a consequence that factors into my accountability.

Key Takeaways: Accountability

- If we escape accountability, we can create destructive habits.
- Enforce accountability for yourself and others in a positive way.
- Accountability is not necessarily negative. In fact, accountability is a positive influence on human action and development.

Consistency

We've now covered self-reflection and how deep our understanding needs to be in order to influence others effectively. To take things a step further, our consistency (or lack of consistency) is something that offers us even more opportunities and advantages to learn from. In our context, consistency means doing something similarly each time you do it. For example, if I show up five to ten minutes late to meetings, one might say, "Brian is consistently late to meetings." Likewise, if I react positively to people at work when they bring me problems, one might say, "Brian consistently handles problems well."

Consistency of words, actions, and even thoughts can lead to habits because if we do the same thing again and again, we can develop a habit. Consistency can be positive, negative, or neutral—all that is needed to call something consistent is that it repeats in a similar way. Commingling our understanding of consistency with accountability can be one of the most powerful lessons in this book.

In our business, we use tools to help us blend these two powerful human actions. Accountability and consistency are purely human traits, meaning that we can control the application of both to effect change in dramatic ways. No other species on Earth consciously controls the accountability of its actions like humans do. While other species can be consistent, they don't think about changing consistent behavior through accountability; thus, humans have a powerful action at our disposal.

We use project management tools to map our projects. We then employ tasks that lead us to milestones. These milestones are a snapshot and measurement of the overall progress of our project, and we use these in combination to be consistent and provide accountability for our team. When we combine the consistent use of our project management system across all the affected people, we are almost certain to reach our goals. When individuals collaborate using the same tool (consistency) and hold each other accountable for the work needed to reach agreed-upon milestones, the results are powerful.

My greatest value to my team and our clients is my ability to map out a project and create the plan needed to reach goals. My ability to provide outsourced accountability while empowering those involved to hold themselves accountable and stay the course to reach our combined agreed-upon goal has provided the most influence on me. My abilities have helped hundreds of thousands of people become the best they can be. But the best examples I have come from my home and teams.

René and I are guilty of spoiling our children; in that, we have been consistent. The level of spoiling has increased from Kristin, our oldest, to Henry, our youngest. However, we have also been persistent in teaching each of our kids the value of follow-through, consistency, accountability, and consequences. In the early years of our parenting, I don't think we used these words, but our actions instilled those tenets with those we influenced.

We empower our children. We give them boundaries and expect them to live within those boundaries, and when they don't, we hold them accountable. We teach them what accountability means, and if the consequence is acceptable, then it's their choice to make.

Kristin moved into our home as a junior in high school. The move for her was very similar to my move from Illinois to California; she moved from rural Texas to urban Colorado. Kristin adapted well to the move and immediately made friends. We tried to provide her the guidance and foundation needed to be a good adult, which was the best we felt we could do with only two years left of childhood. Kristin came to us after 15 years of being parented by her mother and stepfather, who had taken an entirely different approach.

She came to us with few boundaries. She would pretty much get what she wanted. Consequences were inconsistent, but when they happened in her home back in Texas, they were loud and violent. On the other hand, René and I are not yellers. In fact, we don't fight or argue much in our family, and the consequences we impose are more subtle and directed at learning a lesson from our decisions.

Kristin's first test with us was a navel piercing. Her mother and stepfather permitted this without our consent, and Kristin learned a lesson—that she could ignore our position on something and go to her mother and stepfather, thus bypassing our wishes. The next issue was a tattoo. We said "no," but again, her mom and stepfather allowed it. For us, consequences in this instance were difficult. But we knew that the act of defiance was not preparing Kristin for adulthood.

Later, Kristin's mom and stepfather decided to divorce, so that outlet to bypass our disapproval of things was gone. So, Kristin turned to the next available people: extended family.

One day, Kristin's car died. She had failed to maintain it, and it ran out of oil. When Kristin asked us to cosign for a new car, I refused. We had family members who cosigned for Kristin's new car, who then turned to me to help with payments she ultimately missed. These are examples of both consistency and accountability, not only for Kristin but the family members who decided to enable her poor decisions as well.

These issues continued as other family members provided her with money to attend college, where Kristin flunked out. Those family members eventually asked me to repay them—but I said "no." Once again, I did not agree to support poor decisions based on past consistent behavior and a continued lack of accountability; at this point, my family needed to be accountable for their own actions. They provided this help to Kristin and, in doing so, took away her ability to learn lessons. However, they created an opportunity to learn some of their own.

Kristin eventually chose to move back to Texas, where I think she felt accountability would not have been so direct, and she might receive the type of support she felt she needed. But life has a way of circling back around and teaching good lessons. For Kristin, the lesson of consistency began here with some added effort from other family members who decided they were going to take a more vested interest in helping her grow. Kristin's Texas family helped her, but they did so in a more positive and accountable way that still maintained consistency.

Our actions in not bailing out Kristin or my family members had set an example to others, and through our own consistent action, we helped Kristin to address her challenges in a new way that included self-accountability and new positive consistencies.

Kristin was blessed with a daughter shortly thereafter. She pulled herself up and put herself through school. Today, she is married and is amazingly successful in a career that she loves, with a daughter who is beginning to teach Kristin the lessons children often provide to parents: how to be the ones who provide accountability and consistency.

My impression is that Kristin recognized that positive actions proved that making good choices brought rewards, and she began holding herself accountable. Consequences have a way of waking people up. For Kristin, the consequences of the decisions she made for herself eventually woke her to the reality of those decisions *and* the consequences those decisions brought to her; she let down those who helped her, and those people stopped helping her, one bad decision at a time. Once you face the consequences consistently, the message begins to resonate. First, she turned to her mother, then one other family member after another, with each failure helping her see that maybe the original "no" may have been for a good reason. At that point, Kristin understood that our "no's" to her original requests were actually out of love. By learning that my love for her had nothing to do with my duty to hold her accountable, and that my love can't be used to reinforce poor choices, Kristin began holding herself accountable and started making good choices.

Consistency of action and/or decision is difficult to achieve in and of itself, but using consistency to influence change is even more difficult. Saying "no" to a loved one and disappointing them is hard, as is saying "no" to a workmate, peer, or even yourself. However, if you can embrace consistency as a useful tool, you will see change. As with all practices, however, consistency will help you only if you are doing something that is beneficial to self or for the positive influence of others. Consistently doing something that is harmful will result in undesirable consequences. Enter Henry.

Now, I'm not going to tell you Henry has grown into anything negative. Henry is amazing. But I will describe how our family being consistently involved in his life altered *all* our lives—for good and bad.

Henry used to be an amazing BMX rider. He began riding bikes without training wheels at age two and never looked back. He would entertain himself for hours, just riding in circles. When we moved to Oregon, BMX offered him opportunities to improve his natural skills and us an opportunity to keep the kids busy. Henry would beg to go to the track and just ride, and René would take Mary and let him ride.

We did this for three years. We were consistent; we never missed a practice session or race in our hometown or, for that matter, anywhere in Oregon. In fact, as Henry got better and better, our immersion in the sport became a borderline obsession for both René and me. Through it all, we would drag Mary along, setting her up with games and other distractions to appease her as best we could. For three years, this was our life, our choice for our kids *and* for us. We never asked Henry or Mary how they felt about this—we were consumed.

The consequences of this forced consistency were multi-dimensional: good, bad, and ugly.

Let's begin with the ugly. Mary ended up being ignored to a certain extent and she turned to friends who would prove to be emotionally destructive… and potentially worse. She was introduced to Drake, her first boyfriend, who was a couple of years older than her. Drake took advantage of Mary's need for attention. At the same time this was going on, our push to have Henry perform blinded us to the treatment he was receiving from his BMX race team.

One day, this all came to a head when Henry said simply, "I quit." We were shocked back into reality. He hated riding because of the pressure his team and we were putting on him. The amount of pressure he was experiencing would have been a lot for anyone to handle, let alone an 8-year-old.

We identified what was happening to Mary and Henry within a few months of each other. It was a sad testament to what child sports can do to a family. What seemed like consistent time together as a family was actually fueled by the emotional highs when Henry won, not by actually being together. In doing this consistently, we created a vacuum in both our children that was filled with negative issues.

In the end, this lesson about the negative side of consistency, coupled with comfortable focus and being selfish instead of selfless and empathetic, provided us a renewed focus on being together as a family. Over the next few years, we embarked on more focused family vacations. Mary went from a shy and introverted young lady to the captain of her cheer team, and today she is an amazingly successful and productive woman.

Henry has a renewed love of riding bikes. In fact, he played sports but never really embraced one in a fiercely competitive way. Despite his lack of competitive spirit, he ended up with offers to play college baseball. He instead chose a path toward his ultimate dream since age six: to be a Navy SEAL Officer. He attended his freshman year of college on a Naval ROTC scholarship; however, he decided after his freshman year that it wasn't the right path for him.

He decided to stay in college at the same school and is majoring in international management.

Our ability to stay true to our convictions and be consistent has provided something for René and me that is far more valuable than money: respect. Our hope is that we ultimately modeled this for our children through our actions, not just our words.

Key Takeaways: Consistency

- Not all consistency is good. Consistently doing something bad will bring harmful results and undesirable consequences.

- If you can make a habit of bad behavior, you can make a habit of good behavior.

- It's OK to change your mind, and doing so does not change who you are as an individual.

Earning Respect

It is truly an honor when your boss, coworkers, and friends respect you. However, having your loved ones respect you is the next level of honor from such highly regarded figures in your life.

When we lived in Oregon, I lost respect because I felt like I needed to be an asshole to influence the changes that I felt were needed... *and* to make a quick impression that would afford me some attention. When I arrived in Klamath Falls, I emphasized my direct, to-the-point business demeanor, despite the laidback, friendly atmosphere the Klamath business community was known for.

Let me be clear: Being an asshole is not how I want to be remembered by anyone. Respect must be earned, and that takes time. Respect is not a given. It's interesting how other people's perceptions of us can actually change us. I never wanted to be seen as a jerk, but my perception of the environment I was in made me feel like I *had* to be. All too often, I see people demand respect due to their status or perceived significance in life. But the only place this mentality truly works is in the military, where the hierarchy is clearly defined by protocol and procedure.

Early in my own career, I learned that respect was earned. In the military, I was fortunate to be around officers and non-commissioned officers (NCOs) who understood the status of their rank but also understood that they had a responsibility to measure up to that rank. Before I left the Army, I was at Fort Sill, Oklahoma. One day, as I was sitting in the battalion offices, a lieutenant colonel walked by and noticed my 18th Airborne Corp patch and jump boots. He inquired about the patch and my current position, to which I replied that I was leaving the military and was stationed at Fort Sill for my final 45 days. Somehow, he assigned me to him for those remaining days. It's interesting how much power a person with rank (authority) can have, the things an individual can do with that power, and how that power can leave a lasting influence on someone. I had never had someone actively endorse me in such a positive way.

He commanded an Airborne unit that interacted a lot with artillery and was at Fort Sill often to interface with the training facilities there. Over the last 45 days of my military life, I was delegated a lot of menial tasks that supported this officer, and all of them were important to him. He provided me with lists of responsibilities and schedules, then went on to do whatever lieutenant colonels do. His rules were simple: "Be there when I say, always represent the Airborne with your best, and never miss physical training."

While I'm being a tad simplistic about the expectations, this is my takeaway and the perception of how expectations were laid out for me.

The respect he afforded me was kind of a shock, and the respect I had for him never wavered; in fact, I have done work for this man throughout my entire career, and he has helped my team and me become the great professionals we are today. You see, I was an

E3 Private First Class at this time, not an officer or even a non-commissioned officer. The divide between myself and this person was great. However, the influence we had on each other reached past that divide and allowed us to build a relationship that I had never anticipated, as officers and privates don't often become peers in life together.

While respect can take weeks, months, or years to build, it can also be destroyed in a day. I have had my share of destructive moments, too. Over the years, I have had a number of business partners, none of whom are even remotely a part of our lives today. Each season with a partner has left me with an amazing lesson, and none has left me with animosity, jealousy, or anger. In fact, they have mostly given me empathy.

Each partnership offered me challenges that were difficult. At the time I was faced with these challenges, my reactions were fueled by my immaturity and ignorance. Empathy replaced the anger, hurt, and feeling of loss that followed each of these self-destructive reactions to these challenges. The most memorable for me is the second partnership failure I experienced.

Back in 1999, I merged my company with a larger one. After the merger, I owned 33 percent, and my partner owned 67 percent. My partner became a good friend. I looked up to him; I would even go so far as to say he became a mentor. We were very different, however, and at the time, I was a tad too big for my britches. IA was operational in that I was doing ERP work commingled within my responsibilities for our joint company; this work was not in competition, but it *was* in conflict at times, and I was wrong for doing both at the same time.

After 9/11, we were affected like many other companies. During this time, because of my recommendation, we decided to invest in another company a neighbor was starting. We put a lot of effort into this company as well, and it was a big stretch for us. We put our—that is, mostly my partner's—reputation on the line with the bank to make this a go.

Having one partner is tough; having two is amazingly difficult. We were growing fast (seven-figure fast). We did not have the infrastructure required to maintain the growth, nor did we have experience with such rapid growth. Mistakes mixed with greed and arrogance is never a good combination. Needless to say, the partnership fell apart. The new partner got off without ever having to pay my initial partner or me a dime, something that made me really angry for several years. My original partner and I also had a severe falling out. We both ended up financially fine, but not before we both endured tremendous stress and setbacks. The most damaging consequence of all, for me, was the loss of his friendship.

To this day, I miss my original partner. He has become incredibly successful, and I am incredibly happy for him. I split off my original company, and today it also has amazing success, albeit run by the people I hired originally as employees who are now in full control and ownership. However, despite the money lost—millions—and despite the opportunities lost—millions more—the biggest loss I feel today is the loss of friendship and respect I had for both of the people I started these partnerships with. Money is replaceable; respect can be lost for a lifetime. Protect the respect you earn with all you have, and if you can repair damaged respect by being the bigger person, I can't encourage you enough to invest the emotion and time to try.

I have since moved on. Neither of these past partners would extend a hand in greeting today; mine would be left in empty air. I live with a clean conscience knowing that I have paid for my mistakes financially, emotionally, and physically. I also know that when faced with more challenges, I will forever take the high road.

The high road on maintaining respect is my final story. I also had partners in my businesses in Oregon. One of them (for the purpose of this story, we will call him Charlie) is a wildly successful man who had an original partner (we will call him Howard) in his lifelong business. Howard also happened to be one of my business partners. I never met Howard, having only talked to him once on the phone.

When Howard died, his wife was fairly aggressive about wanting to be bought out. During my partnership with Charlie, he taught me about the high road in business. He said, "If you're right, then always follow through regardless of how uncomfortable it is." The best example is how he treated Howard's wife. They owned property together, and when one of the pieces of jointly owned property was sold, Charlie made sure that Howard's wife was paid exactly what was due to her the moment the property sale closed. Even though there were many unsettled liabilities that far exceeded this amount, he never commingled issues. As he put it, "There is no justification for mixing one piece of business with another; they are not connected except emotionally, and that is not enough to put my reputation at stake."

People so highly respect this man that they will do business with him on a handshake. In a time of litigious behavior and an overabundant demand for contracts to define relationships, he can still be counted on to keep his word. This is the ultimate form of respect that I hope to live by. If I give my word, I strive to keep it. If I don't keep it, I would hope it's because I forgot and not because I consciously decided not to do so. If I ever do make such a mistake, I hope to be held accountable and given the opportunity to make it right.

Key Takeaways: Earning Respect

- If you are consistent with your positive influence, you will gain respect.

- Respect can take weeks, months, or years to build, but it can be destroyed in a moment.

- Never allow someone else to pull you back into their negative emotion. Move past lessons learned, acknowledge that failure is the beginning, and hold respect for yourself.

- Extend forgiveness to yourself *and* others in order to gain respect for yourself and from others.

Situational Awareness

Earning respect from others and holding yourself accountable requires something else that is often difficult to maintain: situational awareness. You can self-reflect and identify the things that challenge you and bring you sorrow, grief, and happiness all day, but if you don't practice awareness in the present, nothing will really change.

Situational awareness is living in the present and being conscious about what is happening around you. So many of us go through life on autopilot in comfortable focus; as a result, we miss what is truly happening. However, situational awareness is so much more than just knowing what is going on presently. It's about understanding that our behavior and actions, when inconsistent, will influence things in our lives that will likely give us anxiety. It is understanding how we may react or what we may do in the current situation we are facing. Situational awareness is not just paying attention to outside influence but noticing how we may become influential as a result of what is going on around us.

One area I find that situational awareness is always present is when delegating to my team. I delegate to a fault. However, that delegation does not mean I don't pay attention; there is a difference. If you delegate something that you are ultimately in control of, you must find a way to remain aware of that which you delegated. I'm not talking about micromanagement; I'm talking about finding that one thing that will give you enough situational awareness to feel good about being held accountable for that which you have delegated.

The one thing I don't delegate is accountability to our clients. I maintain enough situational awareness to accept that accountability, which, at times, is not very fun. But I never give up more than I can accept responsibility for, and I always do my best to remain mindful and aware so that responsibility never develops into anxiety.

Being aware may mean keeping tabs on project timelines through dashboards. It may mean having your children check in at certain intervals and meeting their friends in person. It may be that when you enter a new place, you take stock of your surroundings and get comfortable enough to focus on why you're there instead of where you are.

As with most things we discuss, situational awareness is subjective, meaning each person will approach it differently by paying attention to different aspects of their environment to make them feel secure. Every single time we fly, René pays hyper-attention to the safety briefing; me, not so much. However, in my defense, I fly somewhere between 40 and 60 times a year and have for over 20 years, while René flies 2 or 3 times a year. Even though René has flown on a Boeing 737 and Airbus 319/320, she still pays attention. Her situational awareness of what to do if there is an inflight emergency is amazing.

However, if you asked René about most of the people around us, she would not be able to tell you much. On the other hand, I am hyper-focused on the people around me. I want to know who is close to me and what type of people they are. I also consciously tap the seatback of each row between myself and the exit, knowing that should there be an issue, I will just have to tap the seatback that number of times to get back to that exit. I use this habit to bolster my innate situational awareness about how to get off the plane without having to listen to the announcement every time I fly. I have been hyperactive about situational awareness for my entire life. Being situationally aware will also allow you to be somewhat intuitive and will help you remain calm during situations that may become stressful.

As an adult, I have been on two airplanes that have had serious issues. The first was in 1996 when an Airbus plane I was traveling on from Mexico City to Los Angeles decompressed at 36,000 feet. The airplane immediately began a rapid descent, which happened to occur just after some meals had been served. The food all hit the roof, along with a few people. It was chaos.

The people in my row were calm. The lady next to me grabbed my hand and squeezed, and I squeezed back as the airplane did a lazy spiral at a fast rate to a height that would allow us to remove our masks. By the way, the effects of rapid decompression at 36,000 feet feels like someone shoving an icepick between your ears, and you lose the ability to breathe. However, being aware that we were not falling out of the sky and that my seatmates were calm allowed me to remain calm and influence others around me.

This scenario happened again about three months later, on a flight from Denver to Los Angeles; this time, as soon as I could not breathe, I knew what was coming. I used this awareness to remain calm, and, once again, the influence it had on my seatmates was apparent when compared with the actions of others around us who were, quite frankly, losing it.

You can apply this tactic to almost any situation. When I go to my office each day, I try to have situational awareness with regard to my teammates. I look to detect variance in their physical attributes or attitudes. Having this awareness of their well-being helps me to better communicate with them. Using tools to collect data to be situationally aware is also very important.

At IA, we are hired to influence change. We are often tasked with gaining an understanding of the root cause of an issue and then formulating a solution to that issue without upsetting the overall business structure. To accomplish this, we have to be situationally aware of the entire organization. We have developed tools to supply us with situational awareness and be intuitive throughout the process. We call our situational awareness program "BizVision™." However, the principles we use to collect data are basic; we just ask a lot of well-designed questions to understand that which we are being asked to influence.

If you don't know, ask. If something is not clear, ask for clarification. Situational awareness is about gaining clarity and knowing your surroundings as much as possible. The only way to gain this is to be curious and ask questions.

During your quest for situational awareness, you may become aware of things that are just not quite right. Sometimes it's just perspective; other times, it's context. Situational awareness is also knowing if you are being objective or subjective. Just because you like something does not mean it's right, and even though you may be the one in charge, that does not mean you should use your influence to change things you're subjective about. Leaders can often time fall back on "do as I say not as I do." Even when a leader is aware they are violating their own policy, procedure, or even moral standard, they can dismiss their action as a right of leadership. This position ignores situational awareness by setting a poor example and providing an altered situation that others may follow; taking us back to context and perspective. Another example is when we come into contact with a situation, mid-action or mid-sentence. If we don't gain understanding of what was done or said prior to our being involved (situational awareness), we can have a subjective viewpoint that is not correct and take action or say things that are destructive instead of positive.

Key Takeaways: Situational Awareness

- Situational awareness is about living in the present and being conscious about what is going on around you; it only takes a moment to change your life, so pay attention to each moment by staying in the present.

- To be fully situationally aware, you need to have full context and avoid making assumptions through subjectivity.

- Being aware may mean keeping track of a project timeline through a dashboard, having your children check in at certain intervals, or simply acknowledging your surroundings.

Influence

This balance of what we do with our situational awareness leads us to the crux of this book: influence.

Influence is the ultimate responsibility we have as humans. What we do with our influence can dramatically alter the outcome of things we may never even know occurred. Do you think Abraham Lincoln knew that his influence would eventually contribute to the election of our first Black president? Do you think those who invented the written word thought they could influence 7.67 billion humans with a single statement? Or that math would alter the way we look at our world and space?

I could provide enough examples of good and bad influences to write an entire book. However, my goal is not to provide comparisons or tell anyone what is right or wrong. My goal is not to give any (I)individual the tools needed to take advantage in a negative way—we have enough of that going on today. My goal is to make people aware of our opportunity to influence others, hopefully in a positive way.

If we take the time to slow down our life enough to excel in our chosen fields, we can create the opportunity to be respected and thus have a positive influence on those we meet. We all have advantages in this life. Those advantages are individual to each of us. Advantages can affect us individually, or they can affect us as an Individual team. As I've expressed, individual influence is about each of us individually and each Individual moment, task, or team we live through, accomplish, or work with.

We hear a lot about people being individually celebrated, especially in sports. Think about Tom Brady. When you hear about him, you cannot help but be amazed. However, I always wonder, if you put him on the Bears or the Rams instead of the Patriots, would he have the same success? Was his individual advantage that he was part of the Individual team he played with? When you change that team, does the single individual's contribution change? I think it can.

I'm not saying Tom Brady does not deserve credit. He influences his team in a way that instills the drive to be their very best. The owners of the team continue to surround him with players who complement his advantages by bringing out the best advantages of his teammates.

Second Edition Author's Note: The previous statement was in our first edition of this book, released in 2018. We now know that Tom Brady was successfully able to influence the Tampa Bay Buccaneers to win the 2021 Super Bowl. A single person can have tremendous influence and can inspire change in both the individuals and Individuals they interact with. A single person can defy what anyone believes is possible. Never give up on your positive influence. Oh, and we really love when our teachings are exemplified in such a positive and dramatic fashion!

At IA, we strive to create organizations using similar strategies. We help people to understand where they are in the hierarchy; sometimes, that is easy, and other times it requires slowing down. We understand that if we unlock the unique potential in each individual, we can coach them on how to best work with, communicate, and approach other team members, contribute what makes them individual to the team openly and without fear of judgment, and be an overall positive influence. In the end, it's all about identifying the influence and diversity each individual brings to the team. Helping others understand themselves internally and in relation to others will allow them to be their best self and contribute positive influence.

Influence is our greatest responsibility. Influence without accountability can become tyranny. Influence without empathy can become narcissism and totalitarianism. However, influence with empathy and understanding can create a powerful individual who supports a larger Individual with the influence to change lives, directly and indirectly, for a very long time.

As I collect my final thoughts about how you can find your influence, I am struck by the people who have influenced me. I doubt Jack Danger thought he would ever be influential in the writing of a book like this one. I doubt that my ex-partners would think I would be grateful for the influence they had in my life and will be until my dying breath. I had no idea when I started my company in 1996 that I would have three children and a granddaughter and would have influenced hundreds of thousands of people around the world with our BizVision™ process.

When you find yourself struggling with being influenced or influencing others, slow yourself down, be aware of the situation you're in, and try to apply your foundation of self to the problem. Until you learn to slow down and gain control of your influence, internally and externally, this information will only serve as a minor speed bump on your path. You *do* matter, and you matter because you have a unique influence to share with the world. With this realization, you can address any issues in your life that you deem to be negative in order to replace those negatives with positives.

Never forget your "I." Repeat to yourself, "I matter because my *influence* matters." You are *individual* and *Individual*. What you choose to take away from this book will be unique to you since we all learn, perceive, and adapt differently. One constant that I hope you remember is that your influence is your greatest responsibility and your greatest gift, and the best way to control that influence is to slow down. Everything you have learned will hopefully influence you for the better so that you can grow to influence other individuals and Individuals in a positive way. We wish you a prosperous life.

BOOK 2

INDIVIDUAL INFLUENCE: BE THE "I" IN TEAM

Individual Influence: Be the "I" in Team emphasizes that your greatest responsibility is your influence. In *Be the "I" in Team*, you will learn how to be a positive influence and leader for yourself and your teams. The authors, Dr. Brian Smith and Mary Griffin, use real-life experiences as leadership development experts to discuss:

- Being your best self so you can contribute your unique influence

- How to delegate, hold accountable, define values, and find balance

- The benefits of slowing down and staying in the moment

- Remaining humble, mindful, honest, and consistent

- Paying attention to details and investing in self-education

We believe your single greatest responsibility is your influence, and we want to help you have a positive one. By understanding how to be a great leader, you can build, empower, and balance your teams. *Be the "I" in Team* lays the foundation for reaching your and your teams' goals.

Individual Influence: Be the "I" in Team is the second installment of *The "I" in Team* series.

Author Bios

 **Dr. Brian Smith** resides in Algonquin, Illinois with his beautiful wife of thirty years, René, and their two dogs, Maizy and Moose. During the workday, Brian immerses himself in finding business solutions to help his clients succeed (and sometimes this work takes him to riveting locations around the world). His thirty years of business consulting expertise are why many prestigious companies seek his authority on their path to success. Raising a family, starting over fifty successful companies, developing teams, and influencing over eighteen thousand clients in his lifetime has brought Brian prosperity. When he isn't traveling around the globe, Brian enjoys his time reading, cooking, riding his Sea-Doo, being with his children, and spending time with René.

Mary Griffin has a bachelor's in English literature and minored in psychology. She is currently working toward her master's in organizational leadership. In 2014, she started working with IA Business Advisors as an editor. After graduating in 2016, she became a full-time employee and still enjoys working with her team on various projects and developing *The "I" in Team* series to help all current and aspiring leaders find, be, and build their positive influence. In 2020, she became a Kolbe Certified Consultant. Her dog, Bilbo, accompanies her to the office on a hybrid working schedule.

Mary's biggest passions in life are developing others and pursuing social and self-awareness. She has been vegan for seven years and is driven by valuing and promoting diversity. In the words of Neil deGrasse Tyson, "For me, I am driven by two main philosophies: know more today about the world than I knew yesterday and lessen the suffering of others. You'd be surprised how far that gets you."